To Serve As
Jesus Served

TO SERVE AS JESUS SERVED

A Guide to Servanthood

Clem J. Walters

GREENLAWN PRESS

Scripture quotations are from the New American Bible.

ISBN 0-937779-12-1
Library of Congress Catalog Card Number: 83-70964

Printed in the United States of America.

Cover design: Cae Carnick
Cover drawing: Al Warner

Fourth printing

TABLE OF CONTENTS

ACKNOWLEDGEMENTS

Early in the community life of the People of Praise we observed that many people did not know how to, or have a desire to, serve as Jesus served. After several months of prayer and fasting, our Servant School teaching course was developed. This course has been taught to each adult entering our community over the past 10 years. We in leadership have observed the fruit to be good, thus our desire to share this material with others.

I must acknowledge the tireless work of my coworker Jill Boughton, who transformed course outlines and audio cassettes into book form. Without her commitment and skill, this little book would not be a reality.

Additionally, I must acknowledge the fine work of John F. Curran, who in later years taught and refined Servant School. I pray this combined effort gives life to the reader and glory to God.

Clem J. Walters

INTRODUCTION

Jesus then called them together and said, "You know how those who exercise authority among the Gentiles lord it over them; their great ones make their importance felt. It cannot be like that with you. Anyone among you who aspires to greatness must serve the rest, and whoever wants to rank first among you must serve the needs of all. Such is the case with the Son of man who has come, not to be served by others, but to serve, to give his own life as a ransom for the many.

Matthew 20:25–28

DO YOU FEEL CHALLENGED by these words, the words of the one who "came to serve"? Do you think Christians today can still choose to follow the humble example of Jesus? Have you tried to serve as Jesus served and met with failure?

Do you think the kind of work you do has little spiritual value? Do you feel you have no real contribution to make, because others are so much more talented than you?

Would you rather be served than serve others? Do you grumble when you're asked to do something? Do you find it difficult to do a job the way someone else wants it done?

Do you avoid positions of responsibility? When you take a leadership role, are others able to follow your lead, or do they become disheartened and leave you with all the work?

Do you feel "burned out" by too much serving? Does no one appreciate all the work you do or lift a finger to help?

If you answered "yes" to any of these questions, this book is for you. It is designed for any Christian who wants to respond genuinely to Jesus' invitation, "Take my yoke upon your shoulders and learn from me, for I am gentle and humble of heart" (Matthew 11:29). This book is for those of you who have been hesitant about volunteering your services, as well as for you who have exhausted yourselves in apparently fruitless service. Whether you have just begun to serve Jesus or have been serving him for many years, you can become more fully the servant he desires you to be. Through this book, Jesus can equip you to serve your family, your congregation, your prayer group and those in need all around you.

These objectives make little sense to most of the members of a secular society. Why learn how to be an unobtrusive servant instead of a self-assertive achiever? Why obey instead of taking command? Why seek extra work instead of enjoying well-deserved leisure?

Yet you have been created in order to know, love and serve God. Something within you is stirred by Jesus' call to discipleship. You do not comprehend it, but you have seen life come forth through death, resurrection through crucifixion, joy through self-sacrifice. On the other hand, you see the emptiness of a life devoted to self-serving. You experience the truth of Jesus' paradoxical promise, "Whoever would save his life will lose it, and whoever loses his life for my sake will save it" (Luke 9:24).

The teachings in this book follow a traditional pattern. They identify and deal with three obstacles which block your growth as a Christian servant: the devil, the world and the flesh.

First, look at the cosmic picture: Satan is waging a rebellion against God, and you must choose sides between them. It is God's plan that you become a servant like his Son Jesus; his enemy the devil will do everything he can to subvert that plan.

Second, in this book the adjective "secular" denotes what has traditionally been called "the world": not the created order

God instituted and loves, but that system of relationships and values which is hostile to Christ and his kingdom. This system was created by sinful humanity and is now its captor. In each chapter, a contrast is drawn between false values and gospel values. It is important to understand the secular influences which make it difficult for you to become a humble Christian servant.

Finally, you will find anti-gospel attitudes in your own mind and heart, not simply in your school, job and TV programs. These have traditionally been called "the flesh," the weakest part of your nature and the part most liable to temptation. Jesus calls you not simply to change your exterior behavior so that you serve more, but to let him purify your heart so you become a servant motivated by love for him and for all people.

The material for this book came out of a course developed and tested in the People of Praise, an ecumenical community in South Bend, Indiana. Over the past ten years, every adult in this community of over 1,000 persons has heard these same words in Servant School and put them into practice in a variety of situations. The course has enabled individuals to grow in holiness and humility and to work together effectively at many tasks—in putting on dinners for a dozen and conferences for thousands.

These teachings will help you understand and discern the meaning of servanthood as an integral part of discipleship. They will be enlightening to individuals who read this book on their own. However, it is highly recommended as a course of study for churches, prayer groups, etc. Directions and aids for group use are in the appendix. The lone reader may also make use of the discussion questions and assignments designed for groups. These assignments include reflection on scripture passages and other written and practical exercises which will help you apply what you are learning.

CHAPTER ONE

Status or Service?

Jesus, a Humble Servant

ONE OF THE MOST puzzling things about Jesus Christ is the way he behaves. The eternal Son of God, who has all power in heaven and on earth, washes people's dirty feet, the job of a slave (John 13:3–10). Here is a man who knows his position with respect to the whole human race, yet he doesn't push people around or insist on his prerogatives (Philippians 2:3ff.). In fact, when the crowds try to make him king, he hides from them (John 6:15). Here is a unique man who might understandably hold the masses at a distance and insist on their respect, yet we find him rubbing shoulders with outcasts and prostitutes, treating these individuals with respect and not pity.

Jesus identifies himself as a servant—not merely one who performs acts of service from time to time, but one whose whole being is defined by servanthood (Matthew 20:28). The ultimate act of service is, of course, his death and his self-gift to his disciples in the coming of the Holy Spirit (John 10:17).

This picture of Jesus is arresting; it challenges ordinary notions about the way important people behave. Furthermore, Jesus instructs his followers to become humble servants like himself (John 13:12–17). Are you willing to accept this challenge?

5

Servanthood has many benefits for members of the body of Christ. The Lord tells his followers this: When you serve others, you are in fact serving him; in serving the brother you can see, you touch the invisible Lord (Matthew 25:31–46). Some Christians have tried to separate devotion to Christ from service to other people; there is no scriptural justification for this dichotomy. The man who says he loves God but does not manifest love for God's children (James 2:14–17, 1 John 4:20–21) errs as much as the man who attempts to carry out Christ's mandate to love his neighbor without being empowered by the love of God (Revelation 2:1–5).

The Need for Understanding

WHY SHOULD ANYONE take time to read a book about service? Isn't it sufficient simply to accept this vocation? Doesn't everyone already know how to serve?

There is room for every Christian to grow as a servant. It is possible to accept this mission with great fervor and to fall away when it becomes difficult (Matthew 13:20–21). Unless your initial enthusiasm is channeled and disciplined, it will produce little fruit. There is also a temptation to equate Christian service with pastoral ministry. The person who looks simply for a ministry not only overlooks the important contribution of more ordinary forms of service, but runs the risk of assuming pastoral authority before he has sufficient spiritual maturity (1 Timothy 3:6). Practical service is a school in which the character of a leader may most reliably be developed. He who is faithful in little can then be entrusted with greater responsibility (Matthew 25:21).

Values Which Contradict the Gospel

IF YOU TRY to imitate Jesus' example of service, you will encounter opposition from a rival system of values. You may find these values in the structure and rewards of your place of employment, in the heroes and situations presented as normative by the media, and in the constant barrage of advertising which assaults you. What is even more alarming, you may discover that you yourself have unwittingly adopted many of these false values. Do you show more respect to the custodian or to the company president? Do you listen more attentively to the grade-school dropout or to the Ph.D.? Do you seek extra work, or do you look forward to the achievement of additional leisure? Do you resent being forced to do work which you consider beneath your position or intelligence? Do you serve without being asked, or only when the remuneration makes it worthwhile?

Our society is structured around the achievement of status. Service is often seen as a necessary evil, a temporary inconvenience on the road to a position where others can be forced to perform the dirty work. This can be seen in the family, the military, the educational system, the business world. Children in a family do menial work until they mature to sufficient independence to refuse such work. Many students work hard so they can earn degrees which entitle them to more status and less work; different colleges represent different social status. Often, apprentices in a trade are willing to begin at the bottom with grubby work in the hope of progressing to management positions where they can make others carry out their executive decisions.

The man or woman who has arrived is identified by clearly understood symbols and privileges. The position of his desk, the thickness of his carpet, the size of his plants and pictures—all have a particular significance. The higher his position, then, the more value he has as a person; he can expect adulation and deference from his subordinates. His salary is sufficient to insure financial security and happiness, as well as the purchase of more personal status symbols. Money alone, however, is not sufficient to guarantee status; there are jobs, particularly those which entail physical labor, which confer financial benefits but not status on those who hold them. After a certain degree of financial security is achieved, power over others becomes a more important component of status.

It is difficult for the person who has status to view himself as a servant. He is his own master and the master of others. Typically he would associate more menial work with the ranks he has left behind.

It is a commonplace that "you can't get good service anymore." The "service professions" still offer their services for a fee, but there is no service unless a sufficiently high price is paid, and even the professional servant rarely goes beyond the minimum required of him. It is a rare doctor or repairman who will make a house-call, give a free diagnosis, or attend to something he wasn't specifically called in to fix. Service standards are mostly dictated by the market rather than motivated by love for either the work or the customer.

The Implicit Judgment of Status-Seeking

THE EQUATION OF personal and financial worth with status is clearly hard on those who don't make it in the system. But what about those who arrive at the highest echelons of power and prestige? Are they happy? Can they rest secure in their position, or are they constantly defending it against encroachments? How much money is required to buy satisfaction? What sort of persons are they tempted to become? What does power do to those who exercise it? Are people with status free to respond to the real needs of others? How many families have been sacrificed on the altar of advancement?

For the Christian, the pursuit of status has additional dangers. It is based on pride, on the false notion that personal value is earned rather than given by the Creator. It becomes all-absorbing, requiring a singlehearted dedication which is idolatrous. It denigrates the very service by which the Christian identifies himself with the Suffering Servant.

Jesus is harsh in his chastisement of status-seekers who flaunt their positions by the style of their clothing (Matthew 23:5–7). His parable of the landowner erecting bigger barns (Luke 12:15–21) is only one example of how he views the pursuit of security and ostentation. He consistently reproaches his followers for their desire to be the greatest (Matthew 18:1–4). His catalogue of beatitudes promises heavenly reward to those who enjoy no social status whatsoever (Matthew 5:1–12), and he points a warning finger at those who are rich, satisfied and respected (Luke 6:24–26). Even religious acts of mercy are not to be performed for public approbation (Matthew 6:1–4).

The Goal: Spontaneous, Humble Service

THE CHRISTIAN WHO GIVES his life in service to God and to other people should be normal, not exceptional. Daily decisions to be of service should become second nature, spontaneous responses that spring into action without the ponderous weighing of alternatives. When a Christian sees a cigarette butt on the rug, he needn't go through a complex series of deliberations: Who threw that there? Wonder if he'll ever quit smoking! Will anyone else notice it there? Whose job is it to pick that up? Do I have time to take care of it? The Christian servant simply responds to the obvious need, picks it up and throws it away in the proper place.

Remember whom you serve. The sovereign Lord of the universe is free to use his servants as he wills. You are like a member of a corps of chauffeurs assigned to a top-level executive. Imagine that the executive emerges from his downtown office-building with sycophants hanging on his every word. He's on his way out to the airport to clinch a lucrative business transaction. Sitting at the curb is a beautiful, roomy limousine, and lined up on the sidewalk are 10 sharp, well-groomed, intelligent chauffeurs. Each one is trained to drive that car: he can close the door with just the proper touch, shift gears imperceptibly, control the temperature to the executive's liking. The executive walks down the line and says, "You." This chauffeur helps him into the limousine and drives off. The other nine are still standing there at attention, glad they put themselves at the employer's disposal. Nobody cries and kicks and says, "Hey, how about me? I want to drive it!'' If a chauffeur other than the designated one jumped into the car and took off, he would be arrested for car theft. Nor does the chosen chauffeur complain, ''Why don't you pick on somebody else for a change? I have better things to do than hang around the airport waiting for you.'' He simply serves as he is directed. For you as a Christian servant, what matters is the disposition to be of service. Whether or not your services are employed, you are cheerful and submissive.

The Costly Commandment to Become Servants

IT IS NOT EASY to become the kind of servant who is useful and pleasing to Jesus. It won't happen unless you hear Christ's call, desire to grow as a servant, and commit yourself to accept all available grace and to work hard at the task. If this is your resolve, your life will be changed as you read and seek to apply the material in this book. You will learn responsibility, humility and obedience. In addition, you will become more like Christ.

Because much of our society views status as the goal and service as a temporary inconvenience, the Christian servant is liable to be misunderstood. Why doesn't he take advantage of his rights? Why doesn't he act with appropriate dignity? Why doesn't he leave the menial work to others? Why doesn't he insist on his own way when he clearly knows best? Why does he try so hard to do a job the way someone else wants it done? Can't he think for himself? Doesn't he realize he's being stepped on and overlooked?

Jesus offers a simple way to receive such criticism.

> Blessed are you when they insult you and persecute you and utter every kind of slander against you because of me. Be glad and rejoice, for your reward is great in heaven; they persecuted the prophets before you in the very same way.   Matthew 5:11–12

CHAPTER TWO

Pride or Obedience?

True and False Humility

A POPULAR CARICATURE of the humble person is Casper Milquetoast, the man who gets walked on because he lacks the guts to express or assert himself. Terrified, he's sure he can never do anything right, and his conviction is often self-fulfilling. He is henpecked by his wife, manipulated by his children, and stuck with the blame and the unpleasant jobs by his boss and his coworkers.

This is not gospel humility. If you are truly humble, you know your strengths as well as your weaknesses (Romans 12:3–4). You know your place, not the place of a servile wretch but the place of a person called to friendship with your Creator (John 15:15). This is not a partnership of equals; you let God be God and do not try to be the master of your own life. As a competent servant you take cues from your master and make the master's concerns your own. You are not victimized by those who are more assertive than you; rather, you freely choose to put yourself at the service of others, even of those who lack the social status to compel or reward your efforts on their behalf. You respect everyone, giving others' welfare higher priority than your own comfort or preference (Philippians 2:3–4).

Pride, the Pervasive Trap

PRIDE IS the primordial sin of Satan which he successfully employed to seduce mankind's parents. Like Eve, when you succumb to pride you make yourself the measure of all things, judging what is true and good from a self-centered perspective. This rebellion against God's authority takes many forms, and no one is immune to it; you can even be insufferably proud of your own poverty, humility or service.

Pride is closely tied to untruth, to fantasy, delusion, pretense and unrealistic aspirations (Galatians 6:3–4). While pride is often expressed in overestimating your own abilities or importance, it can also take the form of belittling yourself, considering yourself the most klutzy, the least popular, the worst of sinners, someone beneath the reach of God's love. Such judgments are as audacious and unrealistic as the inflated ones more frequently associated with pride.

When you give in to pride, you take the necessary function of self-preservation a step too far, acting as if everything depended on your own efforts and not on the mercy of God (James 4:13–17). You do what you please and are your own boss. You can be flattered by such popular slogans as:

Assert yourself.
You've got to look out for #1.
If you don't toot your own horn, who will?
Put yourself in the driver's seat.
Speak for yourself.
Make up your own mind.
Secure your future.
If it feels good, do it.
I'm going to get mine.

Pride can show up in human relationships as arrogance. When this happens, you may flaunt your position with an ostentatious flourish. You may insist on deference from others, whom you ignore or denigrate. You may be stingy with words of admiration or appreciation, but ready to make others the butt of your caustic humor.

What's wrong with pride? This purported self-sufficiency masks a hollow destitution (Revelation 3:17). Pride is based on a lie which cannot be maintained indefinitely: it denies the reality of your dependence on God and interdependence with others, goading you to advance yourself at the expense of others.

Pride's Pronouncements

EVERYONE KNOWS OTHER people whom this description of pride fits. But what about you as a servant of God? Can you exclude yourself from these ranks?

As you begin to serve God, you will frequently find pride rising within you. Among its utterances are these:

- I have better things than this to do.
- This work is beneath me; my gifts aren't being used properly.
- I'll do it my way; my way is much better than this.
- Why did they ask him to do that? I could do it 100 times better.
- Who does he think he is, anyway?
- I don't need anyone to tell me what to do or how to do it.
- I don't need any help; I'd rather do it myself and make sure it's done properly.
- I can't be satisfied until the job is done perfectly, according to *my* standards.
- I can't be bothered to take time to show someone else how to do it.
- I will do the job willingly as long as it matches my discernment of what should be done and how it should be done.
- I'm the best servant of all. Look how hard I work.

Because you are trying to grow in humility, you can thank God when you recognize pride in such thoughts and attitudes as these. If you admit this pride and look to the example and the transforming power of Jesus, you will begin to notice how the circumstances of your daily life provide many opportunities for you to grow in humility.

The Objective: Obedience and Submission

OBEDIENCE IS, very simply, doing what someone else commands in the way he wants it done. It means putting on his mind, doing it as he directs (I Peter 5:5–6).

In order to understand the value of obedience, you may need to reject the notion of obedience absorbed from the secular culture around you. Those who denigrate obedience often equate it with the mindless, mechanical compliance exemplified by ranks of Third Reich soldiers goosestepping their way to immoral atrocities. Of course, this is not the obedience scripture recommends. As a Christian, you can never comply with a directive to perform evil, or to go against your sincere and well-formed conscience.

However, in most instances you will not disagree with the objective you are given, but only with the style of executing it. In such matters, you can develop humility by deliberately doing as you are told. If your attitude expresses a willingness to learn and to obey, you will be able to find the right time and the right way to make the input that can improve the way a job is done. The proud man interrupts the work of others by raising vociferous objections; the humble man takes his suggestions quietly to the person in charge. The proud man challenges, "What a stupid thing to do!"; the humble man suggests, "Have you thought about doing it this way instead?"

Of course, it is possible for you to carry out another's orders in a legalistic way which does not effect humility. You can do as you are told, all the while muttering about the stupidity of the task. If you are to develop true humility, your heart must grow into the attitude of submission. This attitude is appropriate because you are not a paid employee who owe your boss only a limited amount of time or work; you are a son or daughter who want to become like your Father in thought and feeling as well as in deed (John 15:15).

How can you grow in submission? When you are given an order, do your best to carry it out; furthermore, seek to adopt the leader's evaluation of its importance, so that your own motivation and enthusiasm match his. Even if an order initially makes no sense to you, do not challenge it (''Why on earth should I do that?'') but seek to enter into it (''Could you help me understand why this is a good thing to do?''). Submission of heart is most clearly demonstrated by Jesus' prayer in Gethsemane (Mark 14:32–39). Another good example is the way St. Paul deals with his ''thorn in the flesh'' (II Corinthians 12:7–10). Both Jesus and Paul openly admit their emotional resistance to what is being asked of them, but they leave the final decision to God and refuse to let their feelings deter them from submitting to his will for them.

Growing in Humility Through Obedience

THERE ARE SOME practical steps you can take in order to grow in humility.

Your attitude should be to put others first, to look out for their needs and comfort before your own (Philippians 2:3–4). You clearly demonstrate this attitude when you act as host, giving your guest the place of honor at the table, the choicest piece of meat, the most comfortable chair, and your undivided attention.

As a servant, put yourself at the disposal of others. Be willing to be spent in service, or left unused, like the chauffeur who is not selected to drive the limousine. Jesus' parable of the servant who expects further work rather than relaxation when he comes in from the fields clearly illustrates this attitude (Luke 17:7–10). When you imitate this servant, you expect no congratulations or coddling as a reward for your service. Service has become your way of life, not an extraordinary event for which you must call attention to yourself.

Be eager to serve, and to do the very best you can. If this eagerness does not spring naturally to life within you, ask the Lord to share this disposition with you.

Be eager not only to serve, but also to obey, to do the job as another wants it done, carrying out his orders in detail. If the professor requires a typewritten research paper of 10–15 pages based on secondary sources turned in at 9 a.m., don't go at noon to deliver a 20-page piece of original poetry penned in ornate calligraphy. If your husband wants the children's homework done in ballpoint between 3 and 4, before the TV goes on, and wants to correct it himself, don't decide on your own that 7 to 8, after some vigorous outdoor play, is a better time, that the work should be done in pencil, and that you as mother are better equipped to review it with the children. There is a time for you as wife to give input in arriving at a prudent policy, but, once your husband has set the policy, you can grow in humility by seeing that it is carried out as he wants it done. Of course, there are special circumstances in which you should be flexible, but your orientation is toward obedience.

Check any impulse to complain about your orders or speak against your leader. Obey quietly, like a radio with an automatic tuner rather than one that constantly produces unpleasant static. Be as willing to be taught and directed by other people as you are willing to be attentive to the Lord. "Speak, Lord, your servant is listening" (I Samuel 3:9–10). "Speak, brother; speak, sister, your servant is listening."

Your objective should be to make obedience habitual. Each time rebellion rises up within you, master it and move forward in obedience. As that obedience becomes a habit, you will not have to spend so much energy putting down your negative reaction and squeezing your heart into the right attitude; you will be able to put your energy directly into responding to the command.

It is this habit of obedience that will stand you in good stead when God speaks to you. Because you have practiced prompt and cheerful obedience to lesser masters in relatively minor matters, you will know how to respond to God quickly and wholeheartedly (James 1:21–25).

CHAPTER THREE

Satan's Plan or God's?

The Importance of Daily Decisions

EVERY DAY YOU make countless decisions. Some are so habitual they require little or no deliberation, for instance, stopping for a red light. Other choices are much more deliberate. You may consciously ask yourself such questions as these: Will I get up for my morning prayer or linger in bed a little longer? Will I finish that letter before lunch? Will I leave early enough to be on time for my appointment? Will I have a second piece of apple pie? These are personal decisions for which you are responsible. In each case, you must apprehend the facts, consider the alternatives, weigh the cost and the consequences of each alternative, and choose to act in a certain way.

Such specific decisions can either undergird or erode the umbrella decision you have made about the overall direction of your life. This umbrella decision addresses you in the following terms: Will I follow the Lord Jesus Christ, or will I try to be the master of my own life? Once you have committed yourself to become a servant of Christ and a servant of other people, you must evaluate the effect of each daily, specific choice on your overall commitment. How will it affect your growth as a follower of Christ if you do not respond to a brother's need, or if you set aside your commitment to personal prayer in favor of extra sleep? It is in your daily decisions that you seize or miss your opportunity. Your salvation and the good of the body of believers depend on what you do today—not what you hope to do tomorrow, not what you did or wish you hadn't done two days ago. Today is decisive (Hebrews 3:13, James 4:13–17, Ephesians 5:16, Romans 13:11–14).

The decision to take up service in Christ's kingdom enlists you in a war with a greater theater than your own temporal existence. It is a struggle involving the forces of God and Satan, and peaceful coexistence is not an option (Ephesians 6:10–17). The outcome of the war is assured: victory has been guaranteed by the death and resurrection of the Son of God, who thereby disarmed death, the giant champion of the enemy (Hebrews 2:14–15). However, the residual operation continues on many fronts until the dominion of Jesus Christ is firmly established in every corner of the world. Enraged by his defeat, Satan still acts as if he's in charge, confusing anyone who pauses to weigh his claims (I Peter 5:8–9).

It is not theologically fashionable to talk so clearly about Satan as the personal source of evil in the world. It is often deemed pastorally prudent to shroud the existence and activity of the Evil One in silence, relegating him to the vivid imagination of a more naive age. But this leaves many people defenseless against the evil they are forced to explain away or attribute to themselves alone, surely a grievous psychological burden.

However, the sacred scriptures and the Christian tradition give unequivocal witness to the reality of Satan. Without making him the focus of attention, preachers and spiritual directors through the ages have clearly discerned his work and counseled Christians to resist his enticements and refuse to follow his plan. "Know your enemy" is always sound advice. The Christian looks to Jesus for sustenance, ammunition and direction, but he is sufficiently aware of the enemy's tactics so that sneak attacks do not catch him unprepared.

Salvation History as a Battle

IT IS HELPFUL to take a long view in order to know this enemy. How has Satan attacked in the past? What initiatives has God mounted against him? Where do you fit into this picture?

How did this war begin? Satan started it by challenging God's authority and refusing his own role as a servant-creature. The root sin of Lucifer is pride, the attempt to usurp God's place rather than submitting to his rule (Isaiah 14:12–15). It was also pride to which the serpent appealed in inspiring Eve's disobedience: didn't she want to be like God? (Genesis 3:5). For Adam, disobedience was compounded by the evasion of responsibility, his attempt to fix the blame for his own misdeed on his wife's shoulders (Genesis 3:12).

The history of Israel continues the same story: the people were deceived by Satan's appeal to pride and refused to serve God. The Israelites repeatedly chose to worship gods of their own making and to place their trust in riches and foreign alliances which ultimately disappointed and betrayed them (Jeremiah 2:24–37 and many other places in the prophets).

God's decisive response was Jesus Christ. Jesus did not insist on his divine prerogatives (Philippians 2:5–10). Rather, he identified himself fully with the human condition, assuming not only the place of a creature but also the full consequences of humanity's pride and rebellion (Hebrews 2:14–18). His sacrifice was not accidental. In perfect obedience to the Father, Jesus freely laid down his life to reconcile all creation to God (John 10:17–18). His was not the passive obedience of a weakling; it was the active obedience of a servant of the Most High who acted decisively, honorably.

The victory signaled by the resurrection of Christ from the dead was extended to the church at Pentecost, when Jesus sent the promised Holy Spirit to equip his servants to continue the battle against Satan by reproducing the pattern of his life and death and resurrection (Acts 1:4–5, 8).

Personal Involvement in This Rebellion

YOU MAY BE TEMPTED to view yourself as immune to the allurements of the enemy. However, original sin means that you, too, have within yourself the seeds of pride and rebellion. You can detect these attitudes when you find yourself refusing to serve, when you catch yourself thinking:

I'm not a child; I don't need to be told what to do.

I don't feel like serving; I'm too tired.

That's not my job; let someone else to it.

I'll be glad to do what I'm asked to do but I'm not going to go out of my way looking for work. I'll make myself scarce when volunteers are being sought.

Satan's Plan for Individuals

IF GOD HAS a specific plan for your life, Satan has a bogus plan that opposes God's at every point. You need to know clearly who your enemy is, what his plan is, and which resources of grace are available to oppose him. While Satan's plan for you is unique, his tactics and strategies are universal.

Satan's objective is your damnation and the disruption of God's plan. He can achieve this through pride, the pride which can lead you to refuse your role as a servant of God, choosing rather to live for yourself. The modern word for this kind of independence is "alienation," being separated from your God-given nature and from kinship with God's other children. It is also called "doing your own thing" and "being free." This is a delusive pride based on aspiring to something you are neither made nor meant to be.

Satan's favorite point of attack is what is traditionally called "the flesh," those tendencies to sin and self-indulgence you carry within you as a result of the Fall. With prayerful reflection, you can identify the vices that make you particularly vulnerable to enemy attack: gluttony, greed, lust, laziness, the need for approval, a critical spirit, fear and anxiety, irascibility . . .

(Galatians 5:16–21). These fleshly tendencies can cut you off from God's plan in either of two ways. Sometimes they lead directly to pride, self-assertion and disobedience. At other times, Satan can enslave you through guilt, isolating you through the reverse of pride—considering your sin too grievous for God to forgive (but see I John 1:9–2:3).

God's Plan for His Children

IF SATAN'S GOAL is your defeat and damnation, the Father's plan is your salvation and full incorporation into the body of his Son. In the gospel paradox, Jesus promises that if you surrender your whole life to God, you will find an abundant life you never dreamed possible (Matthew 16:24–26).

The gospel way is not easy, of course. God's plan for dealing with the flesh is death: death to selfishness and sin, death to the fantasies that feed your pride, death to the claim "I can take care of myself; I don't need a Savior," death to the pursuit of every idol which tries to claim the love and loyalty only God deserves (Colossians 3:3–10). This radical death is possible only by the grace which led Jesus to surrender his life for his people.

God's plan is not simply the renunciation of evil but rebirth to new life through the power of the Holy Spirit (Romans 6:4–11). Through the Spirit, you can be comforted. This is not the kind of comfort that soothes away hurts in a protected haven. Rather, the Holy Spirit is sent to guide and direct you. He provides transforming power to live a righteous life. He supplies effective weapons to overcome Satan. It is through the gift of the Holy Spirit that you can be fully incorporated into the plan of the Father, the life of Jesus and visible unity with other Christians (John 14–17, Romans 8). This unity will be manifested in community with other believers where you commit yourself to serve others in a humble, realistic way (Galatians 4:13–14). As you give your life away to your Lord, to your brothers and sisters, you will be transformed into a person who not only acts in obedience to every lawful authority (Romans 13:1) but who also has a heartfelt attitude of humble submission (Ephesians 6:5–7).

Satan detests this service plan; the characteristic words Milton puts into his mouth are "Better to reign in hell than to serve in heaven." He will try to dissuade you from surrendering your life to God, telling you this is suicidal folly, unbalanced in comparison to a more moderate path. But you need only look at the end of Satan's broad, easy road to realize that his pleasures are short-lived, his promises empty, and his warnings unfounded.

The Need for a Personal Decision

HAVING SEEN the historic struggle of Satan against God and examined the plans God and Satan have for you, you must come to a crystal-clear personal decision. Whose plan will you follow? Whose servant will you be? Where is the center of gravity, the fulcrum of your life?

You may be tempted to postpone or evade this decision, to seek a neutral no-man's-land far from the battlefield. But this is a delusion. The battlefield is your heart. Your choice is not whether to be a slave or your own master; your choice is whether to be enslaved to the Lord who created you or to the father of lies, either directly or through giving in to the demands of the flesh (Romans 6:16–19, John 8:31–36).

The decision to follow the Lord goes beyond intellectual assent. It is not sufficient to believe that he exists, that he is good, that he has a plan for your life. You must commit yourself to know, love and serve him personally, to follow his plan, to act in obedience to his commands.

Scripture relates many stories of the vocations of prophets, men and women of God. The call of Isaiah is a good example (Isaiah 6:1–8). When Isaiah encounters the Holy One, his first response is awe and a sense of his own inadequacy. But he hears a very specific question, "Whom shall I send?," and he responds with his whole being, "Here I am, Lord, send me."

Submitting to the lordship of Jesus is an active process. It means giving over every area of your life as soon as it is recognized, actively seeking God's will for the use of time and talents, labor and money, family and friendships, voice and intellect, past, present and future. As soon as you recognize truth, submit your mind to it and incorporate it into your system of beliefs. As soon as you perceive goodness, choose to value, encourage and pursue it. If your emotions do not square with the truth you perceive and the goodness you will, master those emotions rather than being railroaded by them.

Becoming a servant of God is a lifetime project. If you feel overwhelmed by this, you are beginning to learn humility. This must not be a false humility which discourages and paralyzes, but a hungry humility which casts you on the abundant mercy of God. Hungering for holiness, eager to be equipped for battle, thirst for a greater outpouring of the Holy Spirit to energize you with the powerful life Jesus promises all who come to him (John 10:10).

Although becoming a servant of God spans a lifetime, it begins today. You grow in righteousness moment by moment, decision by decision. Every right choice aligns you more fully with God's ongoing plan for your life; every wrong choice makes you more vulnerable to being picked off by the enemy. But in God's plan, even failures and sinful decisions can open up pathways of repentance through which God's cause is advanced in the humble heart.

Resisting Satan

IF YOU HAVE a personal enemy, you also have effective weapons against Satan's attacks (Ephesians 6:10–17). Furthermore, the Lord who lives within you has met that enemy and all his allurements and decisively rejected him (Matthew 4:1–11 and parallels).

How can you deal with areas of temptation and sin in your life? Christian spiritual counsel through the centuries would advise you to assault every problem first as a weakness of the flesh and to submit it wholeheartedly to the lordship of Jesus. This requires humble, persistent prayer, the confession of need for a Savior. Jesus recommends fasting to underscore prayer (Matthew 17:21).

Although you recognize that deliverance comes from God alone, you must also engage yourself in the struggle, taking up the weapons of will-power and discipline, accepting personal responsibility for your sin and taking authority over it. A tested bit of spiritual advice is this from Martin Luther: "Pray as if your salvation depended on God alone; work as if it depended on you alone." Both are true.

An additional weapon may be found by discovering the occasions and circumstances which prompt you to give in to the flesh, and then avoiding or changing those circumstances. If a full carton of ice cream in the refrigerator is an invitation to gluttony, move it to the basement freezer. If a certain group of card partners disposes you to sloth and slander, change partners. If your wife's presence restrains the competitiveness that leads to outbursts of temper, bring her along.

The battle against Satan is an ongoing battle; the enemy continues to work powerfully in the world, and he isn't squeamish about using the most despicable tactics to distract or dissuade you from advancing God's plan to save the world he loves. But never forget that you are enlisted on the winning side and assured of victory in the Lord. As you persevere in the struggle against every form of evil, you must exercise not only patient endurance but also hope, hope which actively expects God's saving intervention and ongoing sustenance to transform you more and more into a servant of God like your brother Jesus.

CHAPTER FOUR

Purity of Heart
or
Substandard Service

Why and How Do You Serve?

Imperfect Motives for Service

BECAUSE YOU LIVE in human society, you are an experienced servant whether you are the mother preparing supper, the sister fetching a diaper, the husband driving his son on his paper route, the clerk waiting on a customer, or the business person preparing a report. However, a careful examination of the motives for service will reveal many which are based on fear, insecurity, ambition and competition for rewards. These motivations may efficiently grease the social machinery, but they do not measure up to the gospel standard, which is purity of heart.

Some imperfect—and often hidden—motives for service are expressed in thoughts such as these:

- If I don't do it, I'll be punished.
- What will others think of me if I don't serve?
- I feel guilty and need to do penance to make up for my failures.
- I'm not much good to anyone; I'd sure like to be useful.
- Serving is a way of getting others to like and appreciate me.
- If I serve well, I can obtain position, status and recognition.
- I want to be noticed, thanked and rewarded for my efforts.
- I want to prove I can do better than he can.

The Gospel Standard: Love of God

SOME OF THE ABOVE motives are more appropriate in a job than in a relationship. In a job, you hope to exchange services for some sort of reward (or the avoidance of some pain). However, the kind of service Jesus commends grows out of personal relationships with God and with other people. The fundamental motive for service must be love. As a servant of God, you do not seek to gain or avoid anything for yourself; rather, you give yourself in service to others.

Jesus sets forth the gospel standard for service in Mark 12:28–34. In this very familiar passage, he declares what God requires of his servants: love of God and love of neighbor.

To love God singlemindedly and wholeheartedly is simply your response to who God is and what he deserves. He is the sovereign Lord of the universe who has invited you into a love-relationship with him. How can you do less than give him back your whole affection, all your desires and energies, thoughts and decisions? He is self-sufficient and needs nothing from you (Psalm 50:9–15), yet he chooses to work through you, respect your freedom, forgive your failures, and accept your worship. How can you continue to view him as a punitive taskmaster or an impersonal dispenser of rewards? Rather, you are the King's servant whose sole desire is to please him by carrying out his will and offering up everything you do for his glory. It is by observing the way his servants are united in carrying out his work that others will come to know this King and desire to serve him as well (John 17:21).

Even when you are serving someone else, you can serve with a pure heart for love of God, as a living sacrifice of worship to him (Romans 12:1–2). This motivation can sustain you in the absence of human recognition and appreciation (Ephesians 6:5–8, Colossians 3:22–25). In fact, you can even rejoice when the lack of earthly rewards promises you treasure in heaven (Matthew 6:2–4, 29–20).

Love of Neighbor

THE SECOND PART of the commandment is equally important. As a servant, you are motivated by love for those you serve. In fact, St. John tells us that any love for God which fails to manifest itself in love for God's children is counterfeit (I John 4:20–21). It is not in paying lip-service to abstractions such as "love of humanity" but in performing specific services for flesh-and-blood individuals that you can effectively manifest your love for God.

This love of neighbor is more than warm feelings that come and go. It is the deliberate decision to serve the other's good. It is the reverent attitude that every person is precious and important. It is the commitment to encourage others, to be their advocate. This decision to be attentive to the value, needs and strengths of others will in turn generate warm feelings. As a loving servant, you don't simply do your duty toward God and neighbor; you are transformed and motivated by the active affection God has toward all his children. But you do not have to mark time until appropriate feelings overwhelm you; you can choose to act in a charitable way.

Growth in Purity of Heart

WHEN YOU DISCOVER that your motives do not measure up to

the gospel standard, you are in position to grow in purity of heart.

First of all, decide to strive for purity of heart, to serve only God in everything you do. This decision can be reinforced by offering your whole life to God in prayer every morning and by pausing before every change of activity to recall again whom you seek to serve in that activity. If you are attentive, you will detect warning signals when your heart has been deflected: Are you hurt, for example, when another person fails to notice and commend your efforts? This indicates that you have become concerned with pleasing men rather than with loving God.

Put your full energy and attention into the job you are given, doing the best you can and confidently expecting God to increase your meager resources and make your work fruitful (Mark 8:4–9). If you are thinking what to do next or wishing you were somewhere else, you will miss the present opportunity to love and serve God.

Implore God to increase your love for all men. Be eager to discover the good God intends and do what you can to contribute to it. If powerless to change your own feelings, draw near to the Father so that divine love can flow through you.

Finally, serve in God's way, expecting no reward. Your business is to serve as well as you can; the results are up to God. If you find yourself wrongly motivated, take specific steps to grow in purity. If you are tempted to seek recognition, look for anonymous ways to serve. If you are tempted to serve for reward, decide to refuse any compensation offered you. If you are tempted to feel inferior, memorize scripture passages about God's love for you and use these truths to repulse the lie that labels you worthless. If you are tempted to compete against another, deliberately advance the cause of your rival.

The Servant's Failings

AS YOU BEGIN to direct your energies toward serving God and neighbor, you will discover character weaknesses which impede your service. These weaknesses are revealed not by examining your interior attitudes but by observing how you act and react in situations which call for selfless service. You can detect a critical spirit, for instance, not by asking, "Am I perhaps too judgmental?" but by noticing the sharp words which come from your mouth.

How often is your service rendered imperfect by laziness, self-indulgence, self-pity or inconsistency? This is your opportunity to assess your strengths and weaknesses so that you can experience the gradual transformation promised in Jesus (II Corinthians 3:18).

Laziness or Diligence?

NOTHING SABOTAGES Christian service faster than laziness. How often do you stand by idle when there is work to be done, either because it's not your official assignment, because you don't feel like doing it, because its difficulty overwhelms you, or because you have more important things on your mind than the humble task at hand? Would you rather be waited on than look after someone else's needs? Do you sometimes stand around waiting for someone to take charge when you yourself could be at work bringing order into a confusing situation? Or do you perhaps set about a task reluctantly, dragging your feet, waiting till you have put in the expected time (whether or not the job has been completed), hoping someone else will do the lion's share of the work. Do you give yourself wholeheartedly to the task at hand, or do you view requests for service as annoying interruptions and impositions? St. Paul's words to the idler are strong and clear:

> . . . when we were with you we used to lay down the rule that anyone who would not work should not eat. We hear that some of you are unruly, not keeping busy but acting like busybodies. We enjoin all such, and we

urge them strongly in the Lord Jesus Christ, to earn
the food they eat by working quietly.

II Thessalonians 3:10–12

You can grow in diligence by developing a servant's eyes. As
a diligent servant, you are not only eager to perform the re-
quested service, but looking for new ways to serve. You do not
simply meet others' needs; you anticipate them. You are never
off duty; you are a servant 24 hours a day, always available to
the Lord and to other people (Romans 12:11, Galatians 6:9–10).
You go beyond the minimum required of you and stick with a
task until it is completed (II Timothy 4:1–2). It is a pleasure for
others to approach you with a request. Instead of grumbling and
making the asker feel guilty for imposing on you, you act
grateful for the opportunity to serve.

Of course, your model in diligent service is Jesus, who rose
early to pray and moved on to meet the needs of the people
around him (Mark 1:32–39). It is he who can sustain you in
your God-given task (Matthew 11:28–30).

Self-Indulgence or Self-Discipline?

YOU CANNOT BE an effective servant of God if you are enslaved
by your own excessive desires, or even by your legitimate
needs. If you are constantly seeking your own pleasure and
relaxation, you will not be available to meet the needs of others.
Many a would-be servant dulls himself to the Lord's voice by
the overuse of alcohol, tobacco, drugs or rich food.

As a perfect servant of God, you must be willing to put aside
your own legitimate needs as well as your excesses. Are you
willing to forego an hour of sleep to intercede when the Lord
awakens you with a need for intercessory prayer? Do you fast in
order to make your intercession more effective? If you practice
deliberate self-denial in these areas, you will be prepared to
meet unanticipated needs, whether they arise at midnight or
noon. St. Paul reminds us of the runner and the athlete always

training themselves in self-discipline (I Corinthians 9:23–27), ready for the contest.

If you discipline yourself through prayer and fasting, you will discover a new attitude toward your bodily needs. Instead of insisting on your right to have these needs and wants fulfilled, you will be able to receive God's generous care for your needs as a gift. If a higher demand intervenes, you can set your needs aside temporarily in order to respond to God's urgency.

Greed or Generosity?

CLOSELY RELATED TO the temptation to be self-indulgent is the temptation to be greedy, not only for money and possessions but also for adulation, appreciation, security and power. Greed shows up in the seriousness with which you pursue the goods you lack and in the way you protect your time, possessions and lifestyle. Service is often inconvenient; it disrupts your comfortable complacency.

As a generous servant of God, on the other hand, you recognize that you are not the owner but the custodian of every gift you enjoy. You gratefully receive the rewards God gives you and eagerly put them at God's disposal. The parable of the pounds (or talents) repeated several times in the Gospels is instructive as you seek to be industrious and reliable with your Master's gifts (Matthew 25:14–30). However meager your resources, you can willingly bring them to Jesus to be shared with others (Matthew 14:16–21).

Scripture contains many admonitions to generosity. "Lay up for yourselves treasure in heaven," Jesus urges (Matthew 6:20). St. James speaks directly to those whose wealth renders them insensitive to their own injustice (James 5:1–6). St. Paul warns the wealthy not to rely on their own resources (I Timothy 6:17–19) and exhorts the Corinthian church to a generosity far more than financial (I Corinthians 8–9). You may be tempted to dismiss such warnings and exhortations because you are not among the wealthy, but greed is a temptation for rich and poor alike, and the tendency to hoard and protect your time and privileges can also intererfere with effective service.

Self-Pity or Cheerful Patience?

MANY DEEDS OF SERVICE are marred by complaining attitudes and words (Philippians 2:14). If you feel misused and put-upon, resentful and sorry for yourself, then your preoccupation with yourself makes it difficult for you to love the Lord or see the real needs of those you attempt to serve. Your energies are drained in asking, "Why do *I* have to do *this*?"

As a servant of the Lord, expect to follow in the footsteps of Jesus (John 15:20–21, I Peter 4:1, Philippians 1:29). Because service cost Jesus his very life (John 15:13), you should not be surprised when service costs you fatigue, discomfort or even pain. Instead, rejoice in this nearness to your Master (Matthew 5:11–12). Endure hardship patiently, fixing your hope on the Lord (I Peter 4:12–19, James 5:7–11).

Irritability or Teachability?

IF YOU FIND every little thing rubbing you the wrong way, you are probably fixed on your own way rather than dedicated to generous service. When things don't turn out the way you expect, you may sulk or complain. You may feel that anyone who dares to correct you must not understand the situation or appreciate your sincere efforts. Meditating on St. Paul's portrait of love in action (I Corinthians 13:4–7) will help to heal you of such irritability.

As a realistic servant, you should welcome opportunities to be instructed and corrected. When things grate on you, look first for the way your own character needs to grow rather than fixing blame on another person or the situation. Be willing to shift gears when it is clear your original plan or assignment isn't working as intended, and be grateful when someone else points out to you how your service can be improved. This teachability will make you a good servant and also a patient teacher of others, open to their suggestions and aware of your own limitations. In Psalm 32:8 the Lord promises direction to those who are humble enough to receive correction: "I will instruct you and show you the way you should walk; I will counsel you, keeping my eye on you."

Criticism or Encouragement?

WHEN YOU ARE working hard, it is easy to become critical of those who set you to work or who work at your side. You may feel they aren't holding up their end of the work. They're doing a shoddy job, making more work for you. Their attitudes are poisoning the atmosphere for everyone else. But such judgments can wind up crippling others, making them give way to discouragement or competitiveness that sets coworkers against one another. If you find yourself acting as a sniper like this, you have given in to pride and may be shielding yourself from correction.

God wants you to be loyal to his other servants as well as to him. He plans to accomplish his work through a body of believers building one another up, not through isolated, individual superservants who make everyone else feel guilty and incompetent (I Corinthians 12:12–27). An atmosphere of mutual help and encouragement inspires everyone to work better and enables each servant to receive the word of correction which is occasionally required (Ephesians 4:20–32). How much more is a child willing to work productively for a teacher who believes in him and commends his smallest effort than for a harsh taskmaster who hovers over him waiting to pounce on the smallest slip!

Instability or Dependability?

SHORT-LIVED ENTHUSIASM will not sustain you through demanding tasks (Matthew 13:20–21). If you serve only when you feel like it, you can never be counted on when the going is tough. If you tend to say yes right away, then forget what you promised to do, your willingness is of little value (Matthew 21:28–31). If you do a thorough job one day and a slipshod one the next, you need to mature into your vocation.

The Lord seeks committed, steadfast servants. With such dependability, you accept assignments willingly. You arrive to begin work on time. You don't put some other concern ahead of your service. You not only begin energetically, but you see the task through to completion. You can be counted on to take responsibility in an unobtrusive but effective way (II Timothy 1:7–8).

Transformation in Jesus

HAVING DISCOVERED the many ways you fall short of the gospel standard for service, what can you do about the situation?

On the one hand, take your failings seriously. The gospel standard is demanding, and it requires a radical selflessness. What you need is not simply a bit more diligence here and a resolution to try harder there, but total surrender to the love and power of God who can renew your heart and make it like his own. It is not natural for anyone to serve as Jesus did (John 13:34); what it takes is a whole "new creation" (II Corinthians 5:17).

On the other hand, resist discouragement. After all, it is God's work to fashion each servant (Ephesians 2:8–10), and his work is careful and unhurried (II Peter 3:9, Luke 13:6–9). He has already brought you a long way and given you the desire for further growth. What he asks is not overnight perfection but a submissive attitude which will permit him to use every event and circumstance in your life to purify you and draw you closer to him and to his perfect plan for you (Romans 8:28–30).

Seek the Lord, then, in words such as these: "Lord, I want to be your servant. I want to be a better servant. I want to do *your* work with *your* strength. Show me how I fail you and which areas of my life you want to begin changing. Help me welcome the light you give me and not be angry when it shows there is still work to be done. Guard me from discouragement. I trust in your mercy to transform me. Show me, also, the specific things I can do to cooperate with your grace at work in me.''

CHAPTER FIVE

Leader or Servant

A False Dichotomy

The Professional Leader and the Perpetual Follower

YOU MAY HAVE one of two reactions to the title of this chapter.

On the one hand, you may be tempted to skip it altogether, thinking, Who, me? A leader? Not on your life! I'm just an ordinary fellow without any special talents. I'm happy to follow directions, but don't put me in charge of anything, please! Let the smart, talented people be the leaders.

But this would be false humility and evasion of vocation.

On the other hand, you may feel gratified finally to have arrived at this point, thinking, Ah, at last a chapter written with me in mind! Enough of this humble, anonymous service! Everyone knows it's the leaders who make things happen, and that's the kind of person I am. Not everyone is cut out for leadership, but I clearly have the gifts to do more than serve as a lackey. It's about time someone recognized that fact.

Of course, this is pride and a misconception of the vocation to leadership.

This chapter has two counterbalancing points which avoid both of the above dangers: (1) You *can* be a leader in some areas, if your heart is right and you are willing not only to use your own gifts but to depend on the Lord and the talents of the Christians working along with you. (2) You *cannot* be the kind of leader God wants unless you are a humble servant willing to follow the direction of others, even those not as gifted as you. Leadership requires more than service, but it builds upon service; in fact, leadership is a particular kind of service you must render to the Lord with purity of heart. The word "ministry" comes from a root that means "service," the sort of service done by a waiter or busboy.

The Need for the Service of Leadership

LEADERSHIP IS an essential service wherever two or more Christians undertake a task together. This is both a practical observation and a spiritual principle.

In practice, work is done much more efficiently if someone takes responsibility to organize the work and keep it moving toward the goal. This need not be a single person; it can be a team of people taking collective responsibility. However, as a team grows in numbers and maturity, it will become clear that making decisions by democratic consensus is unwieldy and impractical. (The decisions in question here are not moral decisions but pragmatic ones. The group may want to discern unanimously what task to undertake, but, once they have agreed upon a goal, it becomes the job of the leader(s) to gather everyone's input and figure out how best to accomplish that goal.)

In the spiritual realm, there is leadership and corresponding obedience at every level. One of Jesus' primary objectives during the three years of his public ministry was to form a group of 12 men to continue his mission (Matthew 13:10–17). Within that band of apostles, Jesus clearly designated a leader (Matthew 16:13–19, cf. Acts 1:15), although he expected all of them to exercise leadership and carefully prepared them for this role both by teaching (Matthew 20:25–28) and example. Thus, when Christians recognize and accept the service of leadership, they are attempting to reproduce God's order.

Mistaken Notions of Leadership

WHEN YOU READ the word ''leader,'' you may picture a ruthless corporate executive who judges everything in terms of personal aggrandizement and corporate profit, a tough military commander who relentlessly drives those under him, or an elected official who abuses executive privilege and distorts truth to his own advantage. Of course, not all leaders in business, the military or public life exercise authority in this way, but the secular system is open to such abuses. You cannot seek or shun leadership based on this model; your model can only be Jesus, leader *par excellence*.

Here are some popular notions of leadership which do not square with the gospel:

(1) Leadership is a function, not a relationship. A leader does a certain job; he relates to his subordinates only to the degree necessary to accomplish that goal. There is a certain mystique associated with important people. In their presence, the underling is tongue-tied and out-of-place. Unless he has a specific question about his work, he has nothing to discuss with the boss. The thought of running into the president on the elevator strikes terror into his heart. The leader's interest in his subordinates is limited to the job they perform; any details of their family life or leisure-time activities remain outside his concern.

(2) The leader is totally in charge; he answers to no one. ''The buck stops here,'' said the sign on President Harry S Truman's desk. Of course, the elected official is ultimately answerable to the electorate; the corporation president to the stockholders. But the times of accountability are infrequent, and the rest of the time the leader can be his own man, enforcing his will on others. In making decisions, he need not seek or even

consider the opinions of those who work under him; he can tell them what to do and, if they don't like it, they're free to leave.

(3) The leader is more important than those under him. His importance is recognized through material rewards and status commensurate with his rank. Others treat him with adulation and deference. This superiority in possessions and status often becomes thought of as moral or personal superiority. The leader is clearly a more valuable person than those lower in the hierarchy; in fact, it may be necessary for him to sacrifice some of them to maintain his own prosperity and eminence. Their jobs and rewards are contingent on his good pleasure.

(4) The leader has power. He uses this power to manipulate others and to force them to serve him. Some leaders (e.g., those in government bureaucracy) do not enjoy great financial rewards; it is the exercise of power which can be the motivating factor for people in these positions. The leader who is infatuated with his own power can use it to dominate and terrorize others. They do the work; he gets the glory.

(5) The leader is best at everything; he does or appears to do all the work himself. It is lonely at the top because this kind of leader must at all costs protect his position by maintaining the fiction that he alone has the talents necessary to perform this function. This kind of leader does not try to develop the talents of those under him; rather, these talents are a threat to his preeminence and are to be discouraged, disparaged or disguised.

Evaluation of Leadership in These Mistaken Modes

EVEN IN HIS OWN value system, this kind of leader is on a dead-end road. He lives in constant terror of being supplanted, losing all his reward in an instant. Perhaps more terrifying than the thought of being fired is the possibility of being "promoted" into obscurity, so that he retains his title but no longer exercises real power in setting directions and making decisions. As a person nears retirement age, this fear can become very real.

More serious than the insecurity of leadership are the moral and spiritual temptations inherent in unchecked power. At the very least, such a leader can become proud and self-centered, measuring everything in terms of his own advancement (Ezekiel 34:1–16). Forgetting gratitude, he can come to believe that he is responsible for his own success, that his status is a right rather than a gift. Because he is obligated to no one, the word "responsibility" can become meaningless to him. He can do what he pleases, answering to no one. In this way, he may miss the opportunity to grow by learning from others, to achieve together with others more than he could attain on his own.

It is a truism that "power corrupts." Pursued to its logical end, the view of leadership as unchallenged power can result in the demonic sort of power exercised by an Adolf Hitler. A leader who sees himself as more valuable than his inferiors may eventually justify exterminating them. Such so-called leadership can dehumanize the subordinates even if they do not wind up headed for the gas chamber. Furthermore, the so-called leader himself can be dehumanized by the way he exercises power. Power comes ultimately from God or Satan. Used in God's way, it is liberating for leader and follower alike. Used as Satan directs, it winds up destroying both (Ezekiel 28:1–19).

Every Christian a Leader

IT HAS BEEN STATED that every Christian can be a leader in some way. What does this mean? A leader is one who through personal initiative effectively inspires and organizes others to accomplish a goal. How can one become this sort of leader?

First of all, be eager to serve the Lord (Romans 12:1–2, I Thessalonians 2:4), because true humility sets no limits on how God may choose to use you. Be willing to be an anonymous servant, but do not refuse to exercise the service of leadership. Let your zeal for the accomplishment of God's will be stronger than your diffidence about your own limitations. The same God who calls you can also empower you to do his will (Philippians 1:6, I Corinthians 1:8–9, II Timothy 1:6–14).

You begin to be this sort of leader when you see a need. Because you have developed servant's eyes, the need will leap out at you. If it is not a need you can meet by yourself, you must work together with others. And if this need is not already someone else's responsibility, you must do something. If you won't take responsibility, the need may remain unmet.

At this point, go before the Lord with the need. Seek God's mind about what should be done and how. Ask if you are the one to do it. Sometimes God will indicate, "No. Be patient; keep praying, and I will raise up someone else to meet this need. Right now I want you to put your energies into this other thing" (See Acts 16:6–10).

But often it will become clear that God is equipping you to lead others in doing something about this need (see Matthew 9:36–10:1). If you accept this challenge and others are willing to follow, you become a leader. This leadership is not often a matter of prominence or great skill. It may mean making phone calls, collecting money, purchasing supplies and assigning specific tasks to others. As you undertake the job, you will learn to do new things and to call on others for needed assistance. In order to be the leader, you do not have to be the most knowledgeable or the most skilled. Rather, your task is to take responsibility for pulling the project together so that others can make effective use of their knowledge and skills.

Remain Under Authority

WHAT CHARACTERISTICS do you need in order to be a Christian leader?

First, you must be a faithful servant, trained and disciplined by service under the leadership of others. You must have a pure heart dedicated to loving God and neighbor, and you must be working to develop the other qualities considered in the last chapter, such as diligence, self-discipline and dependability. But the position of leadership requires more specialized abilities. These gifts may be sought through prayer and developed through practice; few of them are the sort of talents you are either born with or lack. Rather, they are called forth when you are in a position of responsibility, trying to be faithful to the Lord in exercising that responsibility (I Timothy 4:7–16).

When you become a Christian leader, you do not become your own boss; you remain under authority. First of all, of course, you submit yourself to the Lord. But you also submit yourself deliberately to those who have overall responsibility for the area in which you want to work (Romans 13:1). If, for example, you see the need for organizing others in your group to perform a service which has been neglected or done haphazardly, bring your willingness to undertake this service to those with overall responsibility for the group. If you wish to begin a service in your congregation, check with your pastor or elders. Seek not only their permission but also any specific directives they may have. Maintain a working relationship of open communication with them, taking responsibility for decisions they delegate to you and bringing to them decisions which exceed your mandate. In submitting such decisions to them, offer your own suggestions as well, but remember that the last word is theirs. This is very valuable for you as a leader; it enables you to receive the support as well as the correction of your leaders.

Trust in God, Not Yourself

YOUR FIRST RESPONSE to the opportunity to become a leader may be less than enthusiastic. You will not be unusual if your answer is an incredulous, "Who, me?" Perhaps you have a holy fear of the responsibility you are being given, and some distrust of your own ability to discharge it righteously and effectively. However, this reluctance should not prevent you from becoming a leader; rather, it should keep you aware that whatever you achieve will attest God's power rather than your own proficiency.

Scripture records the vocations of many of God's chosen

leaders in dialogues which express this distrust of self and confidence in the Almighty.

Moses asks, "Who am I . . .?" and God counters, "I will be with you." He establishes Moses' credentials with miracles, and overrides his objection of inarticulateness by asking, "Who gives a man speech? Is it not I, the Lord?" God does not deny Moses' limitations or make his task more modest. Rather, he cites his own power to see Moses through (see Exodus 3:10–4:17).

The Lord's dialogue with the judge Gideon is similar. "Go with the strength you have and save Israel," directs the Lord. Gideon demurs, saying "Please, my lord, how can I save Israel?" God simply repeats his promise, "I shall be with you" (see Judges 6:11–24).

Jeremiah's vocation repeats the same pattern ("I am too young." "I am with you to deliver you."), as do Mary's ("How can this be?" "The Holy Spirit will come upon you.") and Peter's ("I am a sinful man." "Do not be afraid.") (Jeremiah 1:4–10, Luke 1:26–38, Luke 5:4–11). In every case, the ground of dialogue is shifted from the qualifications of the leader to the actions and promises of the Lord (I Corinthians 3:5–7).

Maintain the Ideal While Managing the Means

WITH YOUR EYES fixed on the Lord, you should remind others of their primary goal: to love him and to love all men. You must also keep them focused on the specific goal of their project so that they do not become bogged down in subsidiary objectives or substitute means for ends. Although each project has a particular goal, you will have to remind others that the result of their work is in God's hands, not their own. Even a project which fails in its human objective can serve to increase love for God and neighbor (Philippians 1:17–24).

Your job as leader is to provide the materials and direction others need to do a good job. You must organize the work efficiently, using others' talents to the best advantage. You must find the best time for the job, and it is your careful preparation which makes it possible for the time to be used advantageously.

Be Compassionate and Realistic

THE MORE COMPASSIONATE you are toward those who work with you and those you seek to serve, the better leader you will be. This compassion is not a condescension based on pride but a humble fellowship (I Peter 5:1–4). As leader, you must be realistic about the situation and your own limitations. You must know others' limitations and not drive them beyond their ability to follow, though your own example will often inspire them to exceed their preconceived notion of their capacities. Look out for their welfare, protecting them when their own zeal would lead them to ignore their need for rest, food or assistance. Respect others' freedom, refusing to threaten or coerce them (Philemon vv. 8–14); rather, gladly exhort them to be faithful to their commitments (Titus 2:15). Take responsibility to correct others when they fail to do a job properly, or when they manifest an attitude inconsistent with the gospel, but never humiliate the brothers or sisters you seek to correct (II Timothy 2:24–25). Intercede for them and pray with them as you work side by side. Be quick to recognize good work and willing workers with words of praise and encouragement (I Thessalonians 5:14–15). In this atmosphere of mutual encouragement, the body of Christ grows close in love; this love relationship becomes more important than accomplishing a task, though it also has the effect of lubricating the machinery which turns out concrete deeds of love (Ephesians 4:7–16).

Supernatural Qualities of the Leader

BESIDES THESE natural character traits which are developed by patient practice, you can draw directly on the powerful treasury available to you in the Holy Spirit. Exercise expectant faith (Matthew 17:19–20), knowing God's direction and intervention can make your labor fruitful beyond your expectations (I Corinthians 3:5–7). Inspire others to call on God in the same faith-filled way to supply every need (Philippians 4:19–20).

Place your hope firmly in God, and you will find this hope increasing despite setbacks and the death of human aspirations (Romans 5:3–5). Above all, be a lover. Love God wholeheartedly and serve others out of love for them (II Corinthians 12:15, 19; I Thessalonians 2:7–13).

God will give you the spiritual gifts you need to carry out the service of leadership: wisdom and discernment, knowledge and eloquence, miracles and healing (I Corinthians 12:4–12, 27–31). These gifts are not your personal property but the resources God gives you as a leader in the body of Christ. In fact, it may often be others who actually exercise these gifts: as leader, your responsibility is to call them forth and make sure they are used for the good of the whole body.

Jesus, the Unsurpassed Leader

MODEL YOURSELF on Jesus, who perfectly fulfilled every qualification discussed above. He saw man's need and stooped to meet it, inspiring others to follow him in selfless service. He was fully submitted to the authority of his Father (John 8:28–29), compassionate toward all people (Hebrews 4:15), and realistic about the human situation. He respected the freedom of others even when they used it to reject him (John 6:66–71). He wasn't timid about exhorting or correcting his followers (Matthew 16:23), but he was also lavish with words of encouragement (John 16:27). He was solicitous of their physical needs for rest and food (Mark 6:30–32).

Because Jesus not only prayed for his disciples during his time on earth (Luke 22:32) but continues to intercede constantly for every Christian (Hebrews 7:25), you can count on Jesus' power to transform you and the situation in which God places you. If you regularly and deliberately put on the qualities of a servant leader, they will become a well-fitted part of your spiritual life and a valuable asset to the body of Christ.

CHAPTER SIX

Order or Chaos?

The Importance of Scheduling

PREVIOUS CHAPTERS have focused on the servant's attitudes; these chapters were foundational. However, to be an effective servant, you need not only a right heart but also a good plan of action. This chapter presents the tools you should carry in your servant's toolbox and employ to good effect. Of course, you must be careful not to serve the tool but to use it to serve the Lord. With that caution, you will find such tools as scheduling indispensable; the more service you take on, the more essential they become.

As a servant of the Lord, you are employed full-time about your Master's business (Romans 14:7–8). How can you put order into your life so that you actually accomplish what God asks of you and follow through on your good intentions? If you have begun to serve the Lord, you have doubtless seen many of your fine intentions miscarry, either because unforeseen circumstances arose to divert your attention, or because you failed to plan how you would actually carry out your enthusiastic intentions. Meanwhile, time marches inexorably on, and today's opportunity for service escapes.

Unless you work with a schedule for each block of time, you will not be able to accomplish God's work. You probably need a daily, weekly and monthly schedule to provide for your regular and one-time commitments. Even an imperfect plan will enable you to order your life more peacefully than you could manage to do in the absence of any plan at all.

How to Begin Scheduling

WHAT ARE YOUR priorities? You will find it helpful actually to write down goals and objectives for each area of your life: personal goals, goals in your family or living situation, in your church involvement, in your work, etc. If you draw a horizontal line on the paper, you can list the essential goals and commitments above the line and the optional ones—things you'd like to do if you had time—below it.

Now ask yourself, does my actual use of time reflect my avowed priorities? A good way to find out is to keep a detailed record of how you actually spend your time for a week. How much time do you spend at your place of employment? Traveling to and from work? How do you use your time at work? How much time is spent communicating with your spouse and children? When do you spend time with the Lord in prayer? When do you worship with others? When do you serve your church or prayer group? Your family? Your friends? Your neighbors? How much time do you give to recreation and relaxation? To eating, sleeping and personal hygiene? To education? To hobbies? What meetings are regular commitments? What time is unscheduled, and how do you actually use it?

Now, how can you schedule your time to give greater priority to the things you consider most important? If you begin by writing down your fixed commitments (work, meetings and events) for each day, week and month, then you can allot regular time-slots to the things you consider important (prayer, family communication time, service). As you begin to put your schedule on paper, you may discover you are overcommitted and have agreed to undertake more than you can realistically perform. On the other hand, you may be surprised to find there is time available for more service than you thought possible. With such a schedule in hand, you will have a better way of evaluating requests for service than by referring to their subjective appeal or the urgency of the request.

It is a good idea to take time at the beginning of each day and week to set goals and provide extra time for unusual needs. No once-and-for-all schedule can anticipate the special needs and events that will arise. What commitments or deadlines will require finding a babysitter? . . . providing special food? . . . setting aside a block of uninterrupted time? . . . making an appointment? If there is more than one person involved (e.g., in a family or organization), who will take responsibility for doing these things, and when?

How to Plan a Project

AS A GOOD SERVANT you need not only an overall plan but also a careful plan for each specific project you undertake. You have probably had the experience of beginning a job enthusiastically and then being derailed by one roadblock after another that could have been foreseen and prevented. Suppose the task is painting the family room. You arrive at the paint store and realize you don't know what color will go with the furniture and haven't measured the room to see how much paint you need. When you get home with the paint, you have to make repeated trips to the garage and workbench to find dropcloths, ladders, a can opener and a paint stirrer. Then you discover you neglected to clean the paint brushes from the last job and need to buy new ones. After you finally begin to paint, you realize you should have put masking tape on the windows; at this point you must choose between a sloppy job and still another excursion.

Such inefficiency can be avoided by planning each project. The following questions may be helpful:

(1) What needs to be accomplished?
(2) What are the obstacles?
(3) What's the best way to do the job?
(4) What resources are needed?
  (a) What tools or materials are needed?
  (b) What expertise is required?
  (c) How much time will it take?
(5) Do you have the resources to do the job? When, where and how can you provide for those you lack?

How to Grow as a Servant in Your Fixed Commitments

EVERYONE IS LOCKED into regular commitments such as work and meetings. You can simply write off this time, or you can enter into it wholeheartedly as service time. As an employee, you can spend eight hours a day watching the clock and waiting for your real life to begin, or you can do every task at work for the love of God and neighbor. As a committee member, you can put in time at meetings out of a sense of obligation, or you can be fully present and actively seeking God's will for yourself and your organization.

Within fixed commitments, there is often a great deal of flexibility. You may have certain tasks to accomplish at work, but you can often determine the order in which you do them and the time you allot to each. Such decisions are appropriate objects of prayer and discernment. How will you use your breaks and lunch time? To pray and read scripture? To take your son out to lunch? To get to know a fellow employee?

It is important to keep commitments in perspective. God does not require you to live, breathe and sleep your corporation or your organization; he asks you to love him in everything you do. Changes in your circumstances may alter the way you spend your time, but they do not alter your basic vocation as a Christian. It can be helpful to reflect on the following questions: What things in my life would remain constant if I lost my job or had to take a position elsewhere? Am I giving enough attention to these relatively more permanent features of my life?

How to Use Free Time and Resources

YOU HAVE SOME time which is not strictly scheduled and for which you are accountable to no one but God. You may find it revealing to examine your actual use of such free time. Do you use it to serve Satan, to serve yourself, or to serve God and other people? If you were suddenly granted an extra block of time (say, reduction to a four-day work week with no reduction in pay), what would you do with it?

How do you use your extra money, the money which isn't eaten up in paying fixed bills? Whom do you serve with your money? Beyond the commitment (possibly a tithe) to your church, what love-gifts do you freely give to works of mercy? Again, it is revealing to ask "What if. . .?" If you were given $1,000 with no strings attached, how would you use it? What does this reveal about your priorities?

Leisure time is a familiar concept, but what about leisure thought, or daydreaming? What do you find yourself thinking about, wishing for and imagining? Do you spend time on self-fulfilling fantasies? Or do you use your imagination to envision how God's Kingdom could come about more completely?

How to Find the Right Balance

THERE ARE PROBABLY many demands on your time, your money and your attention. Prayerfully consider how you use the resources God has given you, and whether there is a proper balance in your life. Just as three points determine a plane in the physical order, there are three essential ingredients in the Christian life: prayer, study and action. If you spend all your time reading and never put your knowledge into action, you are as lopsided as the person who is so busy doing good that he never has time to communicate with the Source of all goodness.

Prayer

IT IS ESSENTIAL for you to be in regular two-way communication with God. Because he has invited you into a love relationship, it is not sufficient simply to do what he requires; it is your privilege to come to know God as your intimate and life-changing friend. Such friendship demands that the friends spend time together.

Because you have so many demands on your time and energy, it is important for you to make time with God a daily habit, part of your regular schedule. If you pray only when motivated by crushing need or emotion-packed devotion, God will remain a stranger, unable to touch and transform your ordinary daily life. Set aside prime time, time when you are alert and relatively undistracted, and stick to this commitment despite internal resistance and external obstacles.

Reading such treasuries of prayer as the Psalms will give you many models and suggestions for prayer. There you will discover the many facets of personal prayer; worship, thanksgiving, confession and petition are a few. Each aspect of prayer is directly relevant to your vocation to be a servant.

Worship and adoration put things in proper perspective. They remind you whom you serve and how great a master you have. They express your devotion and your desire to serve faithfully. They offer thanks for the many gifts and blessings which enable you to serve at all.

Bring to God your sins and failures, seeking healing for your hurts and forgiveness for your errors. Beg God to continue to transform you into a better servant. Intercede also for those you serve, that as you serve them they may experience their heavenly Father's care.

Everything that matters to a child of God is important to his Father. Nothing is too difficult or too trivial for God. Prayer should therefore be as comprehensive and as natural as conversation with your spouse or roommate. This comparison between human and divine conversation works both ways. It can change the way you speak to God and the way you address the people with whom you live, with intimacy and reverence rather than reticence and ridicule.

Study

IT HAS BEEN SAID that the flabbiest muscle in most adults is their "schoolhouse muscle." If you want to grow in God's image, you must study to learn more about God's world and God's ways. How has God worked with people in the past? What can be learned from his servants who have already walked the way of faith?

The best place to begin observing God in action is in scripture. If you are just beginning a systematic study of scripture, the Gospels are a good starting point, and 15 minutes a day is probably a realistic commitment. Don't be discouraged by passages you cannot immediately understand or apply. If you study God's word faithfully, you will find ample nourishment for your spiritual life.

There is much good literature available to inspire and instruct the Christian servant. Every Christian tradition has its own spiritual classics and heroes of the faith whose biographies trace the action of God in his people. Contemporary testimonies and Christian magazine articles can also shed light on the meaning of Christian service. Finally, a long view and a bit of reflection will enable you to profit from your own experience and the experience of friends who are also seeking to serve the Lord.

Action

THE FOCUS of this entire book is on action, though such service must never be divorced from prayer and study. Be sure you are putting what you learn into practice in the way you serve your family, your employer and your church and/or prayer group. If you are developing a servant's attitude, you will find many practical ways of showing love to those with whom you live, work and worship. Ask the Lord also to expand your contact with others who need and deserve to be served: the poor, the hungry, the elderly, the sick, the imprisoned, the unemployed, the misunderstood and the lonely. Works of mercy on behalf of such people are the test by which Jesus measures his followers' love for him (Matthew 25:31–46).

CHAPTER SEVEN

Secular Work: Christian Service or Necessary Evil?

Scripture and Secular Work

JESUS SPENT MOST of his adult life working as a carpenter. When he began the public phase of his mission, he chose helpers whose professions included catching fish and collecting taxes. Teachers, homemakers and soldiers were frequently found in his company, and he made use of the services of a farmer and a restaurant proprietor during the last week of his life. Within the band of apostles, Judas served as the accountant and the fishermen continued to practice their trade intermittently, with Jesus' encouragement. He instructed his followers to pay taxes and to submit to legitimate secular authority. There is no justification in the life or teaching of Jesus for denigrating secular work.

The early Christian community found it appropriate to consecrate deacons as well as spiritual leaders. These deacons (the word means "servant") were responsible for the material needs of the community. However, their job was seen as a divine vocation which the whole community had to discern and confirm through prayer. The first group of deacons included a servant evangelist, Philip, and the first Christian martyr, Stephen (Acts 6:1–6).

Even the apostle Paul, a full-time Christian servant, took pride in his ability to support himself through being a tentmaker. He strongly commanded every member of the Christian community to earn his own living (see II Thessalonians 3:6–14).

The New Testament is unequivocal in its attitude toward secular work. Work is not only necessary but honorable and blessed by God.

Popular Fallacies and the Christian Attitude Toward Work

MANY CHRISTIANS FORCE a dichotomy between the work by which they earn a living and their real life, which centers on church and family. They see work as a necessary evil, a poor second to Christian service. As a result, the Lord has no effective influence during most of their waking time.

Those who see life in a more integrated way may be tempted to subsume their entire Christian life under their work, or to view their entire work life in spiritual terms.

Of the two, the temptation to make work an idol is more obvious. With the excuse "My work is my way of praying/serving," these workers let their jobs become an obsession which squeezes out other commitments. The threat to family and spiritual life is obvious.

However, it is equally dangerous to overspiritualize one's work. The person who succumbs to this temptation sees Satan behind every difficulty, invokes Christ to mask his own inadequacies, and uses trust in God's providence to excuse him from taking proper initiative to earn his own way. His verbal Christian witness is often rendered ineffective by his careless work habits and condemning attitude toward those with whom he works.

If you are a Christian, service is your full-time vocation. Jesus wants to be Lord 24 hours a day. This does not mean you will always be engaged in spiritual activities; but it does mean the Holy Spirit cares as much about the way you work as about the way you pray.

Special Problems Inherent in Secular Work

THE PREVIOUS CHAPTERS presume a Christian context for service, a context where people are working together to accomplish God's purposes. But most Christians do not spend the majority of their time and energy in such a context. How can the vocation to serve be exercised in a secular context where goals and patterns of relationships may be inimical to gospel values?

You might experience this enmity on several levels. As an employee, you may be expected to engage in practices that violate your conscience as a Christian, such as falsifying records or stretching the truth in order to boost sales. In many cases these issues are gray rather than black-and-white, and the degree of personal responsibility for corporate decisions will vary with your position in the organization.

On another level, you may be troubled by the atmosphere in which you work. Profanity, vulgarity, negative humor, gossip and griping are often standard modes of conversation. You may feel out-of-place, isolated or even persecuted. There is an additional problem—when difficulties arise in relationships at work, others may not know how to work through them with honesty, respect and forgiveness. A small hurt inflicted or received may fester, poisoning your relationship with your boss or a coworker.

Temptations to Wrong Attitudes

YOU MAY BE TEMPTED to adopt many attitudes which are not grounded in gospel values. You must constantly be vigilant against temptations to discouragement on the one hand and pride on the other.

Failure to live up to your own expectations or those of your employer could lead you to question your worth as a person loved by God. Rather than profiting from correction, you could fall into despair. Or you could become so insecure about the possibility of failure that your anxiety becomes paralyzing. Overwork, fatigue and pressure to produce can make it difficult for you to maintain spiritual perspective. Particularly in a routine job, another temptation is to boredom, laziness and lack of ambition or initiative.

Success, on the other hand, has its own pitfalls. Success does not render you immune to anxiety and insecurity about your position. Overweening ambition can become consuming, leading also to overwork and fatigue. If you equate your personal value with your achievements, pride will try to convince you that you alone are responsible for your success. The material rewards that accompany success can become a prime motivator, leading to greed, selfishness and idolatry.

Relationships with others can also be sources of temptation. You may find yourself complaining, grumbling, being critical and disloyal toward your employer. Competitiveness may lead you to blame or slander your coworkers rather than encourage and value them as persons. You may enjoy exercising power over others for personal advantage rather than using legitimate power to effect change for the better.

Putting Work in Perspective

SOMEHOW, YOU MUST keep your work in perspective, finding the right balance between job, family and opportunities for service in church and community. A realistic assessment of your talents and your state in life will help clarify your responsibilities. If you are married, you need to work especially hard toward unity with your spouse in vocational goals; decisions about employment, advancement, education, job changes, travel and transfers must be evaluated in terms of total cost, their short- and long-term effect on a family. Where the career demands of either spouse place the other in an untraditional role (wife as breadwinner, husband with major responsibility for the home), agreement and clarification of expectations are essential.

The Lord's Plan for Each Worker

AS A CHRISTIAN, you cannot peg your value as a person to your performance on the job. While striving for excellence in your work, you must remember that you are created, redeemed and loved by God; this is your security and strength, your resource for handling success and failure alike with graceful humility. Regard every talent and opportunity as a gift God has entrusted to you to use in his service.

Because the Lordship of Jesus extends to all creation and even to those who do not acknowledge him as Lord, you can believe the promise that "all things work together for good to those who love God and are called according to his purposes" (Romans 8:28). You need not blame Satan or bad luck when things at work don't turn out as you had hoped; rather, you can see God's hand, accept God's provision, and seek God's direction in every situation.

Few professions are intrinsically immoral. Unless you are employed as a pimp or a Mafia hit-man, you should probably renounce a quitting spirit and pray for the grace to persevere where God has placed you. There may be a right time for a job change, but you can waste a lot of energy wishing for a more gratifying job, a more personable boss, more flexible hours, or more pay, rather than exercising faithfulness and endurance where you are.

Because you are a child of God placed where God wants you to be, you can bear yourself with presence, dignity and quiet confidence. Your dress and manner should be appropriate, and, when you walk into a room, Jesus should be present there without needing to be mentioned by name.

In discerning the mission God is giving you in connection with your work, be realistic about what you can and cannot do. Don't be content to sit on the sidelines; on the other hand, don't expect to change the world singlehandedly. Aware of your talents and position, do the best job you can; maintain personal integrity in the way you work; influence others by your character, and work for the goal within your sphere of responsibility, whether that be a department, a corporation or a nation.

Because your specific mission differs from that of other Christians, you should avoid guilt or envy about a task given to someone else. Encourage and support those whose vocations are different from your own, and seek to combine forces with them to achieve more than you could by yourself.

Working with Diligence

BECAUSE YOU KNOW that your talents, abilities and opportunities are gifts from God, you are responsible to develop and use them as fully as possible. Do the best job you can, striving for excellence in preparation, performance and progress. There is no excuse for laziness or shoddy work, provided you are placed in a job you are able to perform.

Competitiveness and ambition are not inherently un-Christian. You should want to do your best and to advance to the position where you can be of most service to your employer and where you can have the most effective Christian influence on others. However, examine your motives and your attitude toward other persons; don't denigrate them in order to feed your own ego.

The previous chapter on scheduling is relevant here. Instead of writing off, in effect, eight or more hours a day for work, examine how you use your time at work. Are you giving proper attention to the demands of your job, and to the things within the job which have priority? Are you using your breaks or free time in a creative way?

Motives Make All the Difference

CHAPTER FOUR EXHORTED purity of heart. Whom are you serving and striving to please? Are you seeking to gratify your own ego? Are you burdened by trying to live up to your own unrealistic expectations? Are you always working with an eye on what the boss will think? Do you limit your service to the technical minimum required of you? Do you just put in time with an eye on the clock? Is your concern for coworkers limited to the way in which their tasks intersect your own?

The gospel standard sheds clear light on all these problem attitudes. You are commanded to do everything out of love for God and neighbor. The standard by which this love is to be measured is the totally self-giving love of Jesus. That love constantly convicts, but it also empowers. You yourself are loved unconditionally, and so it is conceivable for you to love God and others in a radical way.

Material Rewards

WHETHER YOU ARE prospering materially or experiencing want, you may be tempted to become attached to the legitimate rewards of your labor. Then your goal becomes financial success rather than the full employment of your talents. Paradoxically, it is often true that, the more money one earns, the more he seems to need. St. Paul's example here is convicting:

> Not that I complain of want; for I have learned, in whatever state I am, to be content. I know how to be abased, and I know how to abound; in any and all circumstances I have learned the secret of facing plenty and hunger, abundance and want. I can do all things in him who strengthens me.   Philippians 4:11-13

The fundamental attitudes for you to cultivate toward material things are trust, gratitude and generosity. Scripture repeatedly urges believers to put aside envy and anxiety, trusting God to take care of every need. Such trust does not excuse laziness; rather, it frees you to work hard, leaving the results to God. When hard work results in financial success, you need not feel guilty or embarrassed; nor should you be arrogant. Receive success as a gift from God and be grateful. Seek God's direction for the generous use of this money to further the coming of his kingdom.

The Christian Employee's Moral Responsibility

SOONER OR LATER, you may encounter conflict between your conscience and the practices of the business world. This may occur on the level of personal integrity, or it may be that the business as a whole is engaged in questionable or downright unethical practices. Particularly if you hold a position of responsibility in your business, you need to pray constantly for clarity and courage.

When you are expected to engage in a practice you consider dishonest—padding an expense account, accepting a bribe, or deceiving a potential customer, for example, pray for a creative alternative. Instead of merely refusing to follow standard procedure, you will often be able to find a more straightforward approach that will achieve the desired results. There may be a time when you must resign rather than engage in wrongdoing, but, if your attitude is humble and prayerful rather than negative and arrogant, you will often be shown a better way.

When the issue is corporate rather than personal wrongdoing, you must pray for wisdom and common sense. If you have been a faithful and diligent worker, you can often use your character and position to effect change, but you must prayerfully discern the right strategy. What is the enemy's plan? Where should you take a stand? What is and is not your responsibility? What are your chances of succeeding? Are you willing to accept the possible personal cost? Is this the right time and way to take a stand? Should you sacrifice a short-term gain in order to get into a position where you can be more effective in the long run? Most important, what is God calling and enabling you to do?

There are no simple answers in the area of business ethics. You must depend on the guidance of the Holy Spirit moment by moment. The battle is today and rests neither on your victories and errors yesterday nor on your fond hopes for tomorrow. If you faithfully seek and follow the Spirit's direction today, God will bring about the results he desires, both in your life and in the morality of the organization.

The Christian and His Boss

As a Christian, you can have a healthy appreciation of power, both the authority your employer exercises over you and the power you may hold over others. Although power is subject to abuse, it is not intrinsically evil, and the Christian can accept and use it to further God's kingdom.

All authority belongs to God and is ultimately derived from him; if you pray "Thine is the kingdom and the power and the glory forever," you can also respect your boss's position and submit to his legitimate authority. Unless you are ordered to commit sin, your stance should be one of obedience, eager to carry out any task you are given (Titus 2:9-10, 3:1). Loyalty to your employer demands that you neither speak nor welcome criticism, even if complaint is the prevailing atmosphere. If you have a grievance, take it directly to the person responsible, along with any positive suggestions for change, and then leave it in that person's hands.

Another corollary of this attitude toward authority is the way you accept the correction your boss may offer. Rather than becoming defensive, seek the truth and try to modify your work accordingly. If you feel you have been unjustly accused, do your best, then rely on God to vindicate you. However, beware of seeing persecution where the criticism is brought about by your own inferior work or bad attitude.

Relating to Coworkers

For the love of God, you are called to serve not only your boss but your coworkers and those who work under you. Your concern for them should go beyond the limits of the job they perform; value them as persons for whom Christ died (Titus 3:2-6). Cultivate relationships; express affection in appropriate ways, and take an interest in them as persons. Pray most faithfully for those you find most difficult to relate to. Be lavish with approval, encouragement and constructive suggestions. Be careful to correct poor work without condemning the worker. When difficulties arise in your relationship with others, handle them in a Christian way, asking forgiveness for your own wrongdoing and seeking to resolve disagreements quickly and charitably. In this, don't be deterred by the fact that your fellow workers may not know how to ask or grant forgiveness in a gracious way.

Don't be surprised when you encounter gossip, backbiting, grumbling, profanity and vulgarity. While refusing to participate in such conversation, be careful not to condemn others, and particularly not to invoke God as their judge. Assume their behavior is motivated by habit rather than malice, and do your best to create a more positive environment. Your Christian presence and example will have a definite effect on others, and you should be ready to give an answer when questioned about your own behavior (Colossians 4:5-6).

Witnessing for Christ at Work

BE EAGER to bear witness for Christ at work. The Lord's mandate to evangelize the world is addressed to you, and his passion for humanity extends to those you encounter as you work. It is no accident that you are placed where you are in the world of work. People who would never darken a church door or pick up a spiritual book can encounter Christ as you work with them or wait on them.

Your most effective witness at work is your character. If you are a diligent worker, an honest person, a loyal employee and one who genuinely cares for others, you will earn a hearing for the good news which has transformed your own life. The way you handle responsibilities, care for others, and respond to pressure will communicate clearly and will often lead to questions which open the way for a more explicit verbal witness.

Seek the guidance of the Holy Spirit for the right time and place to give verbal witness to Christ. Be careful not to steal time from your work in order to evangelize others, nor to cram the gospel down their throats. On the other hand, there is something amiss if you brush off questions about the reason for your cheerful confidence and compassion instead of giving glory to God and introducing others to the Lord. In all of this, you don't have to come across as someone who has it all together. If God is acting in your life in failure as well as success, others will be drawn to entrust their own lives to the Savior.

It is a great support to discover other Christians in your organization or profession with whom you can regularly pray, sharing victories and difficulties. Such relationships often bridge denominational differences and lead to a growth in the appreciation of other Christian traditions. Organizations for Christian athletes, nurses, businessmen, etc., can be very helpful in identifying the specific opportunities and temptations inherent in each profession. Jesus promised never to abandon his followers, and where two or more Christians can claim this promise together, each will be strengthened in his witness.

CHAPTER EIGHT

Hospitality:
Burden or Blessing?

What Is Hospitality?

THINK ABOUT TIMES when you have received hospitality. Your host or hostess was above all a welcoming person who made you feel comfortable and cared for. He may have put considerable time and expense into preparing the home, the food or the entertainment, but what you noticed was the host's interest in you; you may have felt this warmth in the most unpretentious surroundings.

Hospitality, then, is personally welcoming a temporary guest into your environment. It can be as radical a commitment as taking in a stranger in a halfway-house program or as unthreatening as having your child's friend play on the backyard swing set. It can be as elaborate as a four-course banquet or as spontaneous as offering a drink of water to the neighbor collecting for the cancer society.

While people usually associate hospitality with a home setting, a congregation or prayer group can also offer warm hospitality to newcomers.

Examples from Scripture and History

THE OLD TESTAMENT considers hospitality a serious obligation and contains many examples of people who were rewarded for the way they welcomed strangers. Perhaps the most famous guests were the angels who visited Abraham and his nephew Lot (Genesis 18 and 19). Abraham was an eager and lavish host, and his guests brought him God's promise of the birth of a son in his old age. Lot went to great lengths to protect the same angels, risking his own life and family to shelter his guests. In turn, they offered him safe conduct out of a city God was about to annihilate.

In Matthew 10:40 Jesus promises that the smallest act of hospitality will not go unrewarded. Because the early church met in homes to share meals as well as prayers (Acts 2:46), hospitality was interwoven with its whole life. In homes, catechumens received instruction in the faith (Acts 10:38, 18:26-27); the sick and needy were cared for (I Timothy 5:10); traveling missionaries were welcomed (Acts 9:43, 16:15, 18:1-3,7); meals were shared (I Corinthians 11:17-21) and the whole community met to pray (Romans 16:5). The church was not a physical structure or an organization, but a body of people who cared for one another in a day-to-day way.

It is not surprising, then, that the gift of hospitality is listed in the epistles as a qualification for those who are to exercise any sort of leadership in the church (I Timothy 3:2, 5:10, Titus 1:8).

The church in postbiblical times continued to value hospitality highly. Monasteries were not only havens of prayer but also places of refuge for those who had been exiled on political or even criminal grounds. In medieval times, the lord of the castle took responsibility for the safety as well as the comfort of his guests; when guests were expected, the host often sent out an armed party to escort them. Cultures which have been influenced by a scriptural tradition still take hospitality very seriously. How can you leave an Italian home before sharing a glass of wine and a bite to eat? If you refuse, you risk offending your host. This kind of hospitality is still a hallmark of many groups.

Social Obstacles to Hospitality

THE LOSS OF social cohesion in 20th-century America has undermined much of the traditional view of the home as a place of hospitality. Corporate mobility has led to the breakdown of extended families and has discouraged the formation of friendships and neighborhood ties. Even the nuclear family often succumbs to pressure. Families which are themselves broken and hurting are unable to welcome and care for people outside the family.

An atmosphere of relativism may render potential hosts reluctant to impose their ideas or their lifestyle on others. Everything from menu and decor to political and religious opinions is regarded as "fine for me" but worthless or meaningless to others. It takes a certain boldness to be a good host who apologizes for nothing but makes himself and his way of life available to his guests.

Perhaps the most important change has been a shift in the function of the home. Where the home was once the primary locus for work, education, worship, fellowship, protection, and works of mercy, these functions have one by one been stripped away and vested in larger social structures. Protection is offered by the police, not the host, and insurance covers any possible accident. Religious education is entrusted to the church, and secular education is the job of professionals, with minimal parental involvement. Welfare is provided by government bureaucracy and the poor remain anonymous to the average middle-class citizen. Charity is not offered in the home; to practice charity is to write out a check to a philanthropic organization.

This leaves little for the breadwinner or the homemaker to do. Home is a private place where he or she goes to retreat from the responsibilities of the public sector. It is no longer seen as a place where work is done, conversation is lively, learning and teaching occur, people are converted and mature in their faith. Rather, it is a place to lick one's wounds and re-arm for the fray. Letting outsiders into such a private space is exhausting and demanding.

Personal Obstacles to Hospitality

BESIDES THESE SOCIAL obstacles which make hospitality unattractive, you may find many internal obstacles which make you reluctant to extend yourself or your home to others. For example, you may find yourself thinking:

I can't afford to entertain.
I can't be bothered.
I don't want someone to ruin my nice things.
I don't have the time.
I'm inadequate; I don't have anything to offer.
My home isn't nice enough.
I don't know how I'd entertain anyone.
I get all tongue-tied and can't talk to people.
I'm terrified of strangers; I feel comfortable with a few close friends and that's it.
I'm an introvert (or extrovert).
I couldn't take that on; I'm not up to it.

Mistaken Conceptions of Hospitality

SOME OF THESE objections are based on a mistaken but prevalent notion of hospitality as something lavish, expensive and time-consuming. If the purpose of hospitality is to show off or to obligate the guest to repay you, it can indeed be costly. It might require a professional caterer or entertainer, and even this does not free you from attention to hundreds of details of social decorum. The gain expected from such an investment must be great: social advancement, specific favors or the opportunity to promote your favorite cause. At the very least, you hope to be repaid for your troubles by the pleasant company of people you enjoy.

Jesus' exhortation to invite the poor, the crippled, the lame, the blind and those who cannot repay (Luke 14:12-14) is strangely out of place in such a context.

Christian Hospitality

IN ORDER TO understand Christian hospitality, you must focus off of yourself as host to the other as guest. As a Christian host, put aside the motive of personal gain; rather, spend yourself in following Jesus' command to love and serve your guest, making his needs your personal concern. Your home is not your private possession but a gift God has entrusted to you to use in his kingdom. Without making disparaging comparisons between what you have to offer and what other Christians have, put your gifts at the disposal of others. Hospitality grows naturally out of the relationship of brotherhood in the body of Christ. Don't regard your brother's needs as "his problem," but "look on the needs of the saints as your own"; this will prompt you to be generous in practicing hospitality (Romans 12:13). Measure the cost against the generosity of Jesus, who has invited his friends to be at home in his Father's house (John 14:1-7). If you feel at home with Jesus, you will be a gracious guest as well as a generous host (I Peter 4:9-10).

As a Christian servant, then, put yourself and whatever you have at others' disposal. Don't look upon hospitality as an unusual sacrifice but as a normal way of life. You know a divine secret about hospitality: when you open your home and your heart to another person, you are in fact letting in Jesus (Matthew 25:35). The guest may stretch your forbearance or your resources, but every time you extend hospitality, you will discover another facet of the body of Christ.

Preparing the Home

THE MOST IMPORTANT furnishings of the Christian home cannot be purchased in a store. Your home must be an environment where loving relationships flourish and supportive conversation occurs. If those who live with you encourage and care for one another, it will be second nature for you to treat guests in the same way.

In furnishing your home, consider such factors as simplicity and reasonable comfort. Reflect good taste and Christian values in the way you decorate your walls and choose background music. Every family will interpret simplicity differently, but don't let the clutter or ostentation of your home's contents obscure the welcoming presence of Jesus. Provide reasonable comfort in caring for your guest's particular needs. As a considerate host, don't expect an elderly guest to sleep on a cot or a toddler to refrain from touching a fragile knicknack (which could be packed away while the child is around).

Overcoming Obstacles

HOW CAN YOU put to rest those fears and reluctances mentioned above? Begin by scaling down your notion of hospitality: it need not be a lavish affair. If you can't afford a steak dinner, put on the teakettle and offer your guest your undivided attention. If you aren't apologetic about the fare or the surroundings, your guest will feel at home and generously provided for.

The important thing isn't the sumptuousness of the appointments but their availability to the guest. If nothing is off limits to him, he will feel welcome. You can honor a guest in many ways: placing a lefthanded guest at the end of the table, giving him the glass that isn't chipped, offering him the first serving of whatever there is, letting him share his enthusiasms. Remember that the most important thing you can offer your guest is neither steak nor wine, but your care and attention which will be manifestations of the love of Jesus.

Perhaps you do not feel inadequate about what you have to offer to guests; you may be tempted rather to pride and protectiveness. If you find yourself unwilling to risk damage to your possessions, reexamine your attitude toward material things. What is of lasting value, love or crystal? (See I Corinthians 13:1-3.)

Hospitality demands time as well as material resources. Lack of time is probably the most common excuse for not practicing hospitality. However, here again you can scale down your notion of hospitality. If you do not have a whole evening to spend with your guest, enjoy the dinner hour with him before you have to attend to other responsibilities. Hospitality does require setting aside other concerns, but the investment of time need not be a large one. It is also true that practicing hospitality will increase your efficiency in using the time available. A good way to make the best of limited time is to invite your guest to share in the work. Some of the finest conversations occur while host and guest are doing dishes together after an enjoyable meal.

The feeling of inadequacy in time and resources often masks a deeper sense of social inadequacy. You may feel tongue-tied and awkward, especially in conversation with strangers. What can you do about this? First of all, you do not have to entertain your guest by providing brilliant and witty discourse. In fact, a brilliant monologue can be much more boring than a genuine two-way conversation. What are your guest's interests? What questions will encourage him to share about the things that matter to him? What can you share about the good things the Lord has done for you? If you remember what your guest tells you on one occasion, you will be able to ask follow-up questions later: "How is your dad recovering from his operation?" "Did your team win the bowling trophy?" "Is your prayer time going better since you began using that devotional book?"

Sometimes it is the style rather than the content of conversation that needs to be modified. If you aren't sure how you should change, a close friend may be able to suggest that you reduce the volume or stop mumbling, make fewer hand gestures or let others answer questions addressed to them. It is often helpful when a friend or family member agrees to give a subtle signal every time you lapse into the conversational fault which is your biggest downfall.

Moving Ahead in the Practice of Hospitality

HOSPITALITY can be learned. A good place to start is to observe what others do to make you feel welcome. Could you extend the same love and courtesy to your own guests? If you don't know how to do something, ask. How does the mother of a large family prepare enough food for all of them? How does she keep food hot? What can you offer a vegetarian guest? How can small children be included in dinner conversation without having them dominate it? It is helpful for you to talk with other Christians about their successes and failures in practicing hospitality. What worked? What didn't? What can be improved? What are you learning?

The most important way to grow in hospitality is through practice. No amount of theorizing can substitute for inviting a guest over for dinner. Talk with those in your family or living situation about setting aside time on some regular basis for hospitality. Sit down with them and make a list of people you would like to welcome into your home. This will include family members and friends, but what about neighbors, members of your church organization, coworkers, children's friends, those who are disadvantaged in some way? How about people from the local nursing home or foreign students at the local college? Then there are those who can be evangelized by the love of a Christian family. Talk together about what you need to do in order to prepare for a visit in each of these different circumstances.

It is also important to talk with other Christians about the way you welcome newcomers to your services or meetings. Does a stranger feel loved and cared for? Does he know how to participate and what is expected of him? Has he been introduced to others and shown where to find the coatrack, the restroom, a place to sit? Most important, is someone interested in him and why he is there? Everyone in the group should examine his actions and attitudes toward guests. Perhaps it would also be helpful to designate greeters, whose chief concern is making guests feel welcome in the group.

Besides deliberately practicing hospitality, you will grow as a Christian servant if you respond graciously to unplanned hospitality. When the telephone or doorbell rings, you can either be annoyed at the intrusion or you can welcome Christ in the person on the other side of the bell. It is also good to be honest with others about your limitations: "I'm sorry, I can't talk with you right now; can I call you back in half an hour?" or "Would you mind waiting while I get the children started on their homework, then I can sit down with you."

Hospitality can be either spontaneous or planned, but it is a litmus test for servanthood. That is why this chapter is integral to the book: if you avoid the practice of hospitality, you have not yet learned to be a Christian servant.

CHAPTER NINE

Servants of One Another
or
Business As Usual?

The Value of Service for the Christian Body

SERVICE IS VALUABLE for many reasons. Most simply, it is an obedient response to the clear command of our Lord. "Wash one another's feet," Jesus instructed the disciples whose feet he had just washed on his way to the ultimate service of dying for them. "Once you know these things, blest will you be if you put them into practice" (John 13:14-17). "Let the greater among you be as the junior, the leader as the servant" (Luke 22:26). The epistles continue this line of exhortation. "Live as servants of God," St. Peter wrote (I Peter 2:16), and St. Paul stated the other half of the great commandment in these words: "Out of love, place yourselves at one another's service" (Galatians 5:13).

As you begin to exercise the gift of service in your Christian group, you will be able to see the fruit of your obedience. You will see how your service frees your pastors and spiritual leaders to concentrate on their ministry (Acts 6:1-7). You will find yourself delivered from the spiritual stagnation which results from continually taking in the Word of God without putting it into practice (Luke 6:46-49). As you serve along with others, you will find bonds of love and unity growing in a body of believers who can depend on one another in every need, material and spiritual (Ephesians 2:19-22).

Deciding What Service to Undertake

THERE ARE MANY needs going unmet, both inside and outside the Christian body. No single Christian or group of Christians can meet all these needs; to try is to invite frustration and bitterness. If you get bogged down in many good things, you may wind up neglecting the "one thing needful," God's best for you (Luke 10:38-42). Where, then, should you exert your energy?

You can discover the answer only through persistent prayer and discernment. It may come when someone else asks you to serve. It may come when you attempt to serve in one way and meet with failure. If you are actively seeking to know and obey God's will, you will find your place of service.

There are some obvious places of service to investigate. Here are some questions you can ask about your present situation:

• How well am I serving my family or those with whom I live? What more does God want me to do for them? How well am I using my home as a place of hospitality?

• How well am I doing my job, serving my employer and my fellow workers? Does God want me to make any changes in this area?

• What am I doing in my church and/or prayer group? Am I trying to do too many different things? Could I do more? Is there something I should drop in order to serve in a way I am just beginning to see?

• What service am I performing in my community through belonging to other organizations? Should I be doing more, less, or something different? Does the Lord want me involved in a service I haven't considered before? What about my (child's) school or extracurricular activities? What about charitable work in my city or neighborhood?

• Besides organizational commitments, how do I respond to informal opportunities to serve: the neighbor who needs help mowing his lawn or roofing his house, the kids who never seem to have anything constructive to do, the shut-ins I never see?

Have the groups of Christians to which you belong considered God's call to service? Share this book with Christian friends, and consider studying it together. (See Appendix.) Then ask what you could do if you worked together as an action group in your particular situation. Here are some suggestions for Christian groups.

• Are there unmet needs within your church, prayer group or organization? Is there a need for greeters, cleaner-uppers, bannermakers, singers, typists, telephoners or intercessors?

• Should your group be reaching out to others who do not belong to a Christian organization? Does God want you to share the gospel in a more systematic way . . . or to support those who do (e.g., missionaries)?

• What about charitable works? As a group, do you feel called to give specific service to the poor? the elderly? the disabled? the retarded? drifters? beggars? runaways? shut-ins? prisoners? ex-convicts? unwed mothers? orphans? single parents? refugees? the unemployed? the hungry? the homeless? What does God want you to do? As you pray together about the many needs in your immediate environment, what is God putting most strongly on your hearts?

Organizing to Serve

CHRISTIAN SERVICE must be rooted in the love and power of God from beginning to end. Undertake it in response to God's invitation; offer your service for his glory, and leave the results in his hands. The more your group prays together, the better equipped you will be to do God's work in God's way and with God's strength. You can expect God to give you needed direction, to supply additional workers, to clear away obstacles and to change hearts. He does not guarantee you trouble-free service that achieves every end to which you aspire. But he does promise to be with you in all things (Matthew 28:20), bringing his own purposes about, even in apparent failure (Romans 8:28).

With prayer given its proper priority, the next step is designating leadership. Chapter Five presented the need for the service of leadership in the Christian body. Now your group must prayerfully discern whom God is gifting to lead you in this particular task. This is not simply a question of who has the most time or natural talents. Rather, who has the Lord's mind, his vision for this project? Who is willing to see it through to completion? Whom do the others trust so they are willing to give him the support he will need to do this job gladly?

You may be tempted to esteem the leader above the other members of the body; resist this temptation, valuing every task and every gift as essential to the body, holding back nothing which has been entrusted to you. I Peter 4:10-11 expresses it well:

> Like good stewards responsible for all these different graces of God, put yourselves at the service of others. If you are a speaker, speak in words which seem to come from God; if you are a helper, help as though every action was done at God's orders; so that in everything God may receive the glory, through Jesus Christ, since to him alone belong all glory and power for ever and ever.

The leader has a special responsibility to uncover, develop and utilize the gifts of others and to organize them in such a way that they work together harmoniously for the good of all and the glory of God (I Corinthians 12:4-13:1).

On a practical level, the group must clearly specify each

person's job and what is expected of him. Mismatched expectations frequently cause hurt and misunderstanding as well as inefficiency. "You mean you didn't . . .? I assumed you were going to do that!" What tasks need to be done, and who is taking responsibility to do each one? Is there a deadline and a way of recording what progress has been made in achieving these tasks? What should a person do when he discovers he is unable to complete his assigned job? (Give up and drop it? Find a substitute? Report to the leader? Propose an alternative method?)

Talking About Difficulties in Service

AS YOU WORK together with other Christians, you may experience external opposition, friction within the group and reluctance within your heart. It is very important for you to love and trust the others enough to talk honestly about these difficulties and to pray through them together.

What kind of opposition is your group encountering? Should this strengthen your determination to proceed (Acts 4:23-31), or lead you to change your objectives or tactics (Acts 17:5-15)? It is important for your service to be directed by the Holy Spirit in a day-to-day way. It is not enough to receive a goal or a vision from the Spirit; you must also look to him constantly for guidance along the path toward that goal. Having given you an objective, God will not abandon you to your own devices in achieving that objective. He promises his continual presence, strength and direction. The route he chooses may not be at all what you might have chosen on your own.

Friction within your Christian group can be very distressing. Everyone is sincerely attempting to follow the Lord and love everyone else; how can there be such differences? Here again, scripture is instructive. Despite the profound unity of the early Christian community (Acts 4:32), they had fundamental differences to resolve. Acts 14:19-15:35 describes a council convened to settle the question of whether Gentile converts had to follow the Jewish law. Although this question was resolved in an orderly way, a dispute between Paul and Barnabas about whether to give the deserter John Mark a second chance could be resolved only by the two apostles parting company (Acts 15:36-40). Although the reader with hindsight can see how God used this division to multiply the apostles' evangelistic efforts, it must have been extremely painful and puzzling to the early church.

It is important to discuss such differences in a spirit of love and candor, fully explaining your own convictions yet remaining open to the possibility of being persuaded by the convictions of others. In matters which are not essential, one Christian will often give way to another in order to maintain the unity of the body (I Corinthians 10:23-33). It is important to maintain love and respect for another Christian even when you disagree with him, to refrain from personal attack or slander of any sort, and to put a charitable interpretation on every action of another, attributing to him a basic motive of love. "Why did you do that?" can be said in a very condemning way, or with a sincere desire to understand and support the other person. Instead of communicating "What a mean, stupid thing to do!," you can communicate, "I know you must have had a good reason for doing that, and I'd like to understand it."

As you undertake service with others, you will also encounter obstacles within yourself. When you share these in a candid way, they can serve to strengthen the love and unity of the group. It is often helpful to add small-group sharings to the service experience, so people can say things like this to one another:

- "I sure didn't feel like doing that service, so I stayed home. Now I realize that I missed something important."
- "I thought I was too tired to make any contribution, but as we prayed and began to work together, I found my energy renewed."
- "I didn't think through this job well enough to provide all the necessary materials; please forgive me."
- "I don't see how I can find time to take on another job."

- "I'm feeling very resentful right now; will you pray with me so I can give up that attitude?"

A key in this sort of dialogue is to express your own difficulties rather than making accusing statements about others.

Developing Proper Attitudes Toward Service

AS A SERVANT, cultivate right attitudes toward your work and toward those with whom you work.

Commit yourself to do your job the best you can and to improve your ability through practice. Be willing to do anything; no job should be beneath you. Done for the Lord, every job can become a worthy offering. That means you aren't just doing a job anybody could do; you are a worthy member of the body of Christ, offering yourself in service to the Lord and to your brothers and sisters. This attitude gives spiritual value to every task. You serve the Lord when you scrub the floor as much as when you lead the choir.

You may be tempted to place your confidence in your own talents and abilities instead of relying on God. Rather, depend on God from start to finish (Philippians 1:6). You cannot pray unless God's Spirit prays within you, but neither can you wash dishes—even if you've done it 1,000 times before—unless God enlivens your heart with love.

Be teachable and flexible. Give yourself wholeheartedly to the service you are asked to perform, but be careful not to become preoccupied with one mode of serving. If you are asked to drop one form of service and undertake another, don't pine for the familiarity of the abandoned service. Be willing to learn a better way of doing something and to follow the directions of another, even when you think your own way would be preferable.

Cultivating Right Attitudes Toward Other Servants

VALUE EVERY MEMBER of Christ's body, whatever his talents or position. Whether the other person is your leader, your follower or your coworker, he is first of all your brother or sister in Christ, a brother or sister for whom Christ died (Romans 14:15).

Exercise your love for your coworker in concrete ways. Intercede for your brother with the Father (Colossians 4:2). Take every opportunity to commend and encourage your brother in his service (Ephesians 4:25-32, I Thessalonians 4:1-18). "You did a good job there." "Looks like you're working pretty hard." "I like the way you sing while you work." "It's a pleasure to work with you." "Thanks for getting all these materials ready so we could finish the job." If such compliments and thanks do not spring readily to your lips, pray for the spiritual insight to realize how much your brother's service pleases the Lord (Philippians 1:9).

The other side of encouragement is this: refrain from judging your brother, particularly from questioning his motives (Matthew 5:22, 7:1-5; I Corinthians 4:5). Because you are not a perfect servant yourself, you can understand the weaknesses and limitations of others and choose to extend them charity rather than condemnation. Assume your brother is trying to do his best even when the results are less than satisfactory. You can be patient with others because your own confidence is in the Lord. "Please be patient," urges a helpful lapel button, "God is not finished with me yet."

Resist the temptation to be quarrelsome or competitive (Philippians 2:3-4,14). You don't have to outdo someone else to prove yourself the best servant of all. Rather, you are working together for the glory of God, encouraging, assisting and commending one another in your efforts. "Outdo one another," exhorts St. Paul (Romans 12:10) "in showing honor." If you are busy honoring and encouraging your brother or sister, you won't need to insist on your own honor.

Support your leader(s) by your attitude of willing obedience. Like any other brother or sister, the leader needs encouragement when things go right and support when they go wrong. Your attitude can make leadership a joy rather than a burden to the leader (Hebrews 13:17). What a difference between leading someone who says, "Do I have to do *that*?" and someone who says, "What can I do to help?"

Of course, you are not an automaton who follow directions blindly. Your ability to see a better way to do something can be an important contribution to the group. However, learn how to offer this input to the responsible person in a timely and constructive way. When the leader is delegating and explaining tasks, it is confusing and disruptive for you to say, "What a dumb way to do that! Why don't we do it this way?" The time for such input is usually either before the task is begun or after it is completed. If you have made a genuine effort to follow the leader's directions, then you are in a position to take the leader aside and suggest, "Next time, what would you think about doing it this way, for these reasons?" Resist the temptation to complain to coworkers rather than approaching the person in charge. Nothing can poison the working environment faster than stirring up dissatisfaction among people who have no responsibility for changing the situation.

Above all, then, seek to be united with your fellow servants in the body of Christ (Ephesians 4:1-16). Given the choice between working on your own and working along with someone else, prefer fellowship. When obstacles to unity arise, be quick to ask forgiveness and do whatever you can to bring about reconciliation and understanding (Colossians 3:12-15). Together with other Christian servants, seek to develop a common purpose and a united way of seeing things (Philippians 2:1-3), knowing that this is a gift God delights in nurturing among those who join their hearts together in serving him.

Appendix

SECTION ONE

How to Use This Book
as the Basis
for a Course in Servanthood

Teaching the Course

Most Christian groups—families, congregations, prayer groups, etc.—can profitably use this book as the basis for a course in Christian service. This appendix contains suggestions and materials for such a course.

This course on service consists of nine sessions, which follow the nine chapters of the book and which include a teaching and group discussion. In addition, the participants would be expected to be involved in some ongoing work of service. For this reason, the material can best be used with teaching sessions scheduled once a week.

Each session should begin with an opening prayer. For this kind of program, shared prayer and singing is more effective than formal or silent prayer. This should be followed by the teaching, which should last no longer than 45 minutes. The talk should be lively, sprinkled with anecdotes and real-life experiences. Scripture should be the foundation and constant point of reference.

At the end of this appendix you will find outlines for each of the nine talks. The material in the chapters will be useful in writing the talk, although the talk should be your own and should incorporate your own examples, anecdotes, etc.

Questions for small-group discussion follow each outline. Sharing in a small group like this will help the participants apply the material to their own situations, with support from others in the group.

Someone in each group should be designated to keep the discussion on track and to make sure that everyone participates. The session should end with another time of prayer, either in the small discussion groups or in the large group. It is particularly important to pray that God effect a change in the hearts of all present so that they might learn to serve as Jesus did.

Finally, this appendix includes a daily assignment for the week following the teaching. These assignments include reflection on scripture passages and other written and practical exercises which will enable the participants to apply what they are learning.

Practical Points

The material of the course cannot be assimilated unless it is put into practice. Of course, the participants should seek to apply the teachings to their home life, job and other activities, but the group must also experience structured service as a group. The leader should determine the nature and the extent of this service. It should be hard work. I suggest approaching your pastor or the leader of your organization. Ask him how your group can be of service. Tell him you are not looking for the sort of service that requires pastoral gifts or results in public prominence; the more menial the job assigned, the better. Are there chairs to be set up? song books to be collated? a storage room to be cleaned out? spring cleaning to be done? Have him specify how he wants the job done, and pledge yourselves to carry out his directions as diligently as possible. The service should be spread out over the duration of the course so that reflection on it can be part of your growth together. Some groups may choose to incorporate service into each meeting, having an hour and a half of teaching, discussion and prayer followed by an hour of service. Others may want to have shorter meetings each week for teaching and several longer sessions of service at a different time, perhaps on Saturdays. The total time of the course shouldn't be spread out more than three months.

If you are unable to organize service for the group as a whole, ask each participant to select his own service, subject to your approval. This service should be direct and unglamorous, something which develops humility rather than tempting to pride, something which serves a particular person or institution. For example, cleaning the church bathrooms would be better than heading the parish maintenance committee, helping a family in the ghetto preferable to supervising a collection of food for the needy. Taking a retarded child out for an outing would contribute more to the objectives of the course than being president of the local United Way drive.

The commitment to service will be costly. It will require setting aside other good activities which have a legitimate claim on the participants' time. But, unless this investment is made, the value of the course will be minimal.

At the outset, it is essential that each participant be committed to this course and clearly understand what is required: faithful attendance, punctuality, note-taking, homework and practical service. Each requirement has its own rationale; taken together, they put the participant in the position of deliberately being a servant who does not determine his own hours, way of listening or assignment. He may experience feelings of rebellion at the way things are being handled; but this is a chance to grow in humility.

Keep a record of attendance and punctuality for both teachings and practical service. If a participant feels he must be absent, he should not simply inform the instructor, but submit the reason for his absence in advance, leaving the final decision to the instructor. Only a very serious reason should excuse a person from this commitment. If the reason is serious enough, permission to be absent should be given graciously, not grudgingly.

It is important for everyone to decide at the beginning to do his best, not only to perform what is asked of him but to enter into it wholeheartedly. This is especially true of the service assignment. The job assigned may have no apparent value in building up the kingdom of God. The student can probably think of a hundred better ways to use his time: feeding the hungry, reading scripture, spending time with the family, getting enough sleep. . . . If the work is of actual service to the church or prayer group, this is a side benefit; its chief purpose is to be a school of humility and character formation. The harder he works at doing the best job he can for love of God, the more effective this training will be.

SECTION TWO

Talk Outlines
Discussion Starters
"Homework"

PART TWO

Status or Service?

Talk Outline

Objective

To motivate the participants to lay aside the pursuit of status and learn to become humble servants like Jesus.

Teacher Outline

I. This course will train you to serve and imitate Christ in a down-to-earth way.
   A   Christ was a humble, willing servant.
   B.   In serving those you can see, you serve Christ.
   C.   Your initial enthusiasm needs to be disciplined for maximum value.
   D.   Practical service is foundational for pastoral ministry.
II. Many of the values prevalent in society challenge gospel values; you have probably absorbed some of these false values.
   A.   Secular society values status above service. Service is viewed as a necessary evil in the climb to positions of status.

B. The achievement of status is signaled by symbols and privileges, money and power.

C. Once status is achieved, one refuses to do work that is beneath that status.

D. Service is seen as a commodity which can be bought.

    1. Such service is motivated by money, not love.

    2. The quality of service seems to be degenerating.

III. Jesus clearly condemns the pursuit of status as a false value.

A. For those who make it to the top,

    1. Success is neither satisfying nor secure.

    2. They can be corrupted by power and blinded to the needs of others, even their own families.

B. In terms of status, those who don't make it to the top are often considered failures.

C. It interferes with Christian commitment and contradicts Christ's teaching about service.

IV. Becoming Christ-like servants is costly.

Discussion Starters

1. What do you hope to gain from this course?
2. Share an experience of serving or being served that helped you grow in your Christian life.
3. Where have you encountered wrong attitudes toward status and service? How are you tempted to adopt these attitudes?

"Homework"

1. John 10:17-18—Read and meditate on Christ's free, courageous decision to be a servant, laying down his life out of obedience to his Father and love for you.
2. Read Isaiah 42:1-9, 49:1-7, 50:4-6, 52:13-53:12. What is the servant of the Lord like? How did Jesus fulfill this picture of the chosen servant? Think of examples from his life. How are you called to do the same?
3. John 13:1-17—Prayerfully read the passage. Imagine the scene. Hear the Lord's exhortation, "Wash one another's feet." Let him speak to you about what it means to be served and to serve in the body of Christ.
4. Read James 1:9-11, 2:1-13. Imagine yourself in this little example. Would you honor the rich man above the poor? Ask Jesus to give you his attitude toward the lowly.
5. Matthew 25:31-46—Prayerfully read the passage. Who are the "least of these my brothers" in your life? Which ones have you refused to serve? Which ones can you decide to serve this week?
6. Decide on one practical thing you can do to serve someone— write a letter, make a visit to someone in a nursing home, prepare a gift, invite a guest, share clothing. . . . Write down what you plan to do.

Pride or Obedience?

Talk Outline

Objective

To recommend obedience as an effective antidote to pride.

Teacher Outline

I. Defining terms.
  A. Humility is
     1. Not a poor self-image or conscious condescension.
     2. But realistic apprehension of God, yourself and others.
  B. Pride is
     1. A challenge or rejection of God's authority.
     2. The fantasy of pretending to be what you are not, aspiring to what you are not intended to be.
     3. A perversion of self-preservation.
     4. Aggressive arrogance toward others.
     5. Pervasive. A problem for everyone, and as slippery as Jell-o.
     6. Pernicious and divisive, denying your need for others and the Father.

II. Learning humility through obedience.
  A. Obedience is
    1. Adherence to another's command.
    2. Responsibility, not mindlessness.
  B. Submission goes beyond actions to attitudes and motives.
  C. Obedience can be learned.
    1. Put others first.
    2. Be at the disposal of others.
    3. Regard service as ordinary without expecting a reward.
    4. Be eager to serve well.
    5. Be eager to obey.
    6. Avoid grumbling.
    7. Make obedience habitual.
    8. Learn to obey people so you will be able to obey God.

Discussion Starters

1. Share about a humble person you've known.
2. How are you tempted to be proud?
3. Have you experienced the freedom of obedience through your practical service in this course?

"Homework"

1. Read James 4:13-17. How do you manifest this pride of self-sufficiency?
2. Luke 18:9-14—After reading this passage, write a prayer the "Pharisee" in you might say. Now write your own prayer as a "publican" and pray it from the heart.
3. Philippians 2:1-16—Prayerfully read the passage. Meditate on the humility with which Christ emptied himself to become a servant. What does it mean for you to imitate him?
4. Read Luke 17:7-10. Imagine yourself as a servant in this situation. Is there any room for pride? What rebellious attitudes rise up in you? Do you deserve a reward for your service?
5. Read 1 Peter 5:5-6. Meditate on how to "clothe yourself with humility." What opportunities have you had this week to choose deliberately to obey? Write down some examples.
6. Psalm 131—Pray this psalm slowly and reverently.

Satan's Plan or God's?

Talk Outline

Objective

To present the rival plans of God and Satan so that the partici-pant can make a genuine personal decision to follow Jesus.

Teacher Outline

I. Your decisions have cosmic import.
   A. You make countless daily decisions.
   B. These decisions are ways of carrying out your basic decision to become a servant of the Lord.
   C. Your choice for the Lord involves you in a battle.
II. There is much to learn from salvation history.
   A. Satan refused to serve God.
   B. Human beings followed Satan's lead in rebelling against God.
   C. God sent Jesus to be perfectly obedient, freely laying down his life to reconcile all creation to the Father.
   D. Jesus sent the Holy Spirit to equip you in the battle.
   E. You are personally involved in Satan's rebellion.
III. There are two plans vying for your allegiance.
   A. Satan's plan
      1. His objectives: your damnation and the disruption of God's plan.

      2. His weapon: pride.

      3. His ally: your flesh.

      4. His ball and chain: guilt.

  B. God's plan is for you to

      1. Die to yourself.

      2. Live for the Lord.

      3. Be committed to serve others.

IV. Because these two plans are in opposition, you need personally to reject Satan and enter into Jesus' plan.

  A. Whom will you serve?

  B. This personal commitment goes beyond intellectual agreement.

  C. Actively submit to Jesus' lordship in every area of your life.

      1. Conform your intellect to the truth of God's word and wisdom.

      2. Choose goodness with your will.

      3. Take charge of your emotions.

  D. Grow in righteousness through specific prayerful choices in today's battle.

      1. Begin by struggling against every problem that is a weakness of the flesh.

        a. Pray and fast.

        b. Exercise will-power and discipline.

        c. Change tempting circumstances.

      2. Persevere in hope.

Discussion Starters

1. Where in your life do you clearly see the confrontation between God's plan and Satan's plan?

2. Where have you experienced Jesus' victory over evil?

3. How does Jesus want to extend his Lordship over you?

"Homework"

1. Revelation 11:15-12:17—Read through the passage prayerfully, noting the death struggle between God and Satan and the strong assurance of Jesus' victory.
2. Genesis 3:1-24—Read the passage prayerfully, putting yourself in the place of Eve. How does Satan appeal to your pride? What decisions in your life have sprung from pride and rebellion against God?
3. John 8:23-59—Read the passage prayerfully, noting the clear opposition between the servants of God and the slaves of the devil. Write down the characteristics of Jesus in contrast to the traits of the Evil One. Whose child do you want to be?
4. Read Romans 6:16-23. Whose slave are you? With what result?
5. Read Ephesians 6:10-20. How extensive is the battle described here? Are you adequately equipped? How can you take up and use these weapons?
6. Read Isaiah 6:1-8. Imagine yourself with Isaiah in this scene. Let God's majesty cause you to kneel down before him in worship. How will you respond to his call?
7. Keep a record of the choices presented to you this week, concrete examples of the opposition between God's plan and Satan's plan for your life.

Purity of Heart
or
Substandard Service

Why and How Do You Serve?

Talk Outline

Objective

To help the participant test his motivation against the standard of purity of heart and to detect weaknesses of character which hinder his service.

Teacher Outline

I. Why you serve—growing in purity of heart.
- **A.** You have many imperfect motives for service.
- **B.** Jesus gives two right motives for service, both based on personal relationships:
  - **1.** Love of God.
  - **2.** Love of neighbor.
- **C.** You can grow in purity of heart.
  - **1.** Decide to serve God alone.
  - **2.** Give it all you've got.
  - **3.** Pray for God's love for all people.
  - **4.** Serve in God's way.

II. How you serve.
- **A.** Take stock of the character weaknesses which impede your service.
  1. Laziness.
  2. Self-indulgence.
  3. Greed.
  4. Self-pity.
  5. Irritability.
  6. Criticism of others.
  7. Instability.
- **B.** Cultivate new attitudes in place of the above.
  1. Energetic diligence.
  2. Self-discipline.
  3. Generosity.
  4. Cheerful willingness to suffer patiently.
  5. Teachability.
  6. Encouragement and loyalty.
  7. Steadfast dependability.
- **C.** Have confidence in God's power to transform you.
  1. Realize how radical this transformation is.
  2. Exercise faith in God's transforming work.
  3. Take action as God reveals how you can cooperate with his grace.

Discussion Starters

1. What characteristics of a servant struck you as most important and/or most needed in your life?

2. What specific decisions can you make to become a better servant?

"Homework"

1. Mark 12:28-34—Read the passage prayerfully. Imagine someone asking you the scribe's question. How would you answer? Let Jesus' reply speak to your heart, and respond to him.
2. Ephesians 6:5-8—Reflect on this passage addressed to slaves. How can you serve the Lord wholeheartedly in all you do? Where do you find yourself working rather for human approval?
3. Read I Corinthians 13:1-13. Do you manifest love as you serve? List the qualities of love (vv. 4-7).
4. Read Philippians 2:12-16. How do you measure up as a servant?
5. Read James 1:23-25. Let this word exhort you to action.
6. Read I Corinthians 9:23-27. Are you going "all out" to serve the Lord? What discipline does this demand?
7 List one example of how you have been called upon this week to exercise:
   a. Diligence.
   b. Discipline.
   c. Generosity.
   d. Cheerful willingness to suffer.
   e. Flexibility, teachability.
   f. Encouragement, loyalty.
   g. Dependability.

Leader or Servant

A False Dichotomy

Talk Outline

Objective

To present leadership as a particular kind of service for which the Holy Spirit equips the Christian.

Teacher Outline

I. Leadership is an essential form of service, not the opposite of service.

II. Mistaken notions of leadership are prevalent.

    A. What are these notions?

        1. Leadership is a function, not a relationship.

        2. The leader answers to no one.

        3. The leader is more important than those under him.

        4. The leader has power over others.

        5. The leader does everything himself.

    B. This kind of leadership can result in:

        1. Insecurity.

        2. Pride.

        3. Evasion of responsibility.

        4. Loneliness.

        5. Sin.

III. You can be a Christian leader, one who through personal initiative effectively inspires and organizes others to accomplish a goal.

    A. You become a leader when you:

        1. Are willing to serve the Lord.

        2. See an unmet need you cannot meet alone.

        3. Take responsibility to lead others in accomplishing a goal.

    B. Cultivate these qualities (in addition to the characteristics of a Christian servant found in Talk IV):

        1. Natural, learned traits:

            a. Humility.

            b. Trust in the power of God.

            c. Idealism.

            d. Organization.

            e. Compassion.

            f. Realism.

            g. Concern for others who may be working too hard.

            h. Abhorrence of coercing others.

            i. Intercession.

            j. Willingness to exhort others, to correct others when necessary, and to encourage others when they do well.

        2. Supernatural traits which inspire and energize others:

            a. Expectant faith.

            b. Hope.

            c. Loving service.

            d. Openness to spiritual gifts.

    C. Model yourself after Jesus, the unsurpassed leader.

Discussion Starters

1. What leaders have inspired you? How did they do it?
2. Do you have negative feelings about being a leader or being led? Why?
3. How can you grow in Christian leadership?
4. How can you help your leader(s)?

"Homework"

1. Mark 6:7-13, 30-44—Observe Jesus in action caring for his disciples and the crowd. Prayerfully meditate on the example of his leadership. Imagine you are one of the Twelve. How would Jesus lead you and form you as a leader of others? Let him continue that work in you.

2. Read Matthew 23:1-12. How does this picture of the "leaders" of Jesus' day contrast with Jesus' call to his followers? How are you tempted to pride of leadership?

3. Read Matthew 20:20-28. How is status in the kingdom related to service? Meditate on the example of humility and service Jesus gives.

4. I Corinthians 12:4-31, 14:1—List the ministries in the body (v. 28) and the gifts (vv. 8-10). What ministries and gifts have you been given? What ministries and gifts does your body of believers need? Intercede for God to raise up people with these gifts.

5. II Corinthians 4:1-15—Prayerfully reflect on this description of a Christian servant/leader. Through it, let the Lord exhort you. List the qualities of a Christian leader from vv. 1 and 8; vv. 2, 3 and 7; vv. 10-11; v. 13; v. 15.

6. I Timothy 3:1-13, 4:6-5:2—List the qualifications of the bishop (leader). Which ones does the Lord want you to work on developing?

7. II Corinthians 11:7-12:10—Meditate on Paul's portrait of himself as a leader. What does it mean for a leader to be "weak," following the way of the cross?

Order or Chaos?

Talk Outline

Objective

To give the participant tools which will make every part of his daily life more productive.

Teacher Outline

I. Schedule your time.
   A. Why schedule?
   B. How to schedule:
      1. Set priorities and carry them out.
      2. Schedule planning time.
      3. Use your schedule as a servant, not a master.
   C. Plan specific projects carefully.
      1. Determine the need or objective.
      2. Ascertain the obstacles.
      3. Plan
         a. What to do.
         b. How to do it.
         c. Resources needed.
II. Grow as servants in your fixed commitments.

III. Use your free time to serve God.
  A. Leisure time; how do you spend it?
  B. Extra money; how would you use it?
  C. Leisure thought: what occupies your daydreams?
IV. Grow as servants who live a balanced life.
  A. Pray daily.
  B. Study how God works with people.
  C. Serve in action and word.

Discussion Starters

1. How has planning helped you be a better servant?
2. What areas of your life need to be submitted to the lordship of Jesus?
3. How can you make better use of your time and resources?

"Homework"

1. Divide a piece of paper by drawing a line across the middle. List commitments which you must do above the line; below the line things you like to do. Include responsibilities to yourself (eating, sleeping, hygiene, relaxation, hobbies); to God (church, prayer); to family (meeting time, family prayer, recreation, housework); to others (meeting, visiting, letters); to your employer.

2. Keep track of the way you actually spend your time this week. How much time is allotted to things above the line? Below it? Do you spend most time on your highest priorities?

3. Where do you need to make adjustments, to limit time spent on "x," schedule time for "y"? List specific changes you will make.

4. Romans 13:11-14:11—Read the passage prayerfully. Now pray through your day, yielding everything you do to the lordship of Christ.

5. Commit to paper a plan for a specific service project.

6. How would you spend $1,000 of unexpectedly received money? Does your actual use of money reflect what you count as most important?

7. List some things you daydream about. List things that would be good to imagine, think about, or chew on—scripture passages you don't understand, areas of Christian life you need to grow in, etc. What books might help? How about memorizing scripture?

Secular Work:
Christian Service or Necessary Evil?

Talk Outline

Objective

To help the participant see how he can serve the Lord in his place of employment even though his coworkers don't share this explicit objective.

Teacher Outline

I. Introduction.
    A. The New Testament places a high value on secular work.
    B. Common fallacies:
        1. Secular work is excluded from the lordship of Jesus.
        2. Work should be all-consuming.
        3. Work must be seen in purely spiritual terms.
    C. The Christian attitude: Being a servant is a full-time vocation.
II. Secular work presents special problems.
    A. External problems:
        1. Immoral practices.
        2. Atmosphere.
        3. Relationship problems.

 B. Internal problems: wrong attitudes
   1. Negative experiences:
    a. Failure, discouragement.
    b. Overwork.
    c. Anxiety, insecurity.
    d. Boredom.
    e. Laziness.
   2. Temptations based on success:
    a. Pride.
    b. Greed.
    c. Ambition.
   3. Wrong relationship to others:
    a. Disloyalty.
    b. Domination, competitiveness.

III. You can approach your work as a servant.
 A. Keep your work in proper perspective.
 B. Know that Jesus is in charge.
   1. Find personal value in his redeeming love; bear yourself with dignity.
   2. Learn how to react to failure.
   3. Be content where you are.
 C. Strive for excellence in your work.
 D. Check your motivation.
 E. Cultivate the right attitude toward material things as God's gift.
 F. Pray for moral courage, wisdom and integrity.
 G. Be sure your work relationships are right.
   1. Respect the position and authority of your boss.
   2. Care for those who work with and under you.
 H. Witness in words and action.

Discussion Starter

1. What is the most difficult problem you as a Christian face at work? What is God teaching you about how to deal with this problem?
2. How can we better support one another in our vocations?

"Homework"

1. Acts 6:1-7—Read the passage prayerfully. Why were servants (deacons) needed? What were their qualifications? How are you being asked to serve as a "deacon" where you work?
2. Read II Thessalonians 3:6-15. What does Paul's exhortation and example have to say to you about diligence? Your attitude toward others?
3. Read Ephesians 5:8-21, 6:5-18. What specific advice does Paul give to employees and employers? What parts of his more general exhortation seem to apply most to your work situation?
4. Matthew 6:19-34—Let this passage speak to you about confidence in God who provides for your needs. What could you do to express this confidence? (Perhaps sacrifice some personal pleasure or purchase in order to spend extra time and/or money directly in God's service.)
5. List and pray for those with whom you work. Ask God how to pray for each one and what attitude you should have toward him or her.
6. Keep track of how you spend your work time during one day. Are you giving high priority to the right aspects of your job? How are you using break time? Did you have any choices to make today under the guidance of the Holy Spirit?

Hospitality:
Burden or Blessing?

Talk Outline

Objective

To encourage participants to practice hospitality with greater frequency, skill and expectancy.

Teacher Outline

I. Hospitality:
  A. Welcomes a guest temporarily into your environment.
  B. Is practiced in churches as well as in homes.
II. Scripture and history underline the importance of hospitality.
III. Prevalent secular attitudes undermine Christian hospitality.
  A. Social problems and attitudes make hospitality difficult:
    1. People are rootless.
    2. Many families are broken.
    3. Lifestyles are seen as personal and relative.
    4. People expect social agencies to meet others' needs.
    5. Homes are seen as private places of refuge.
  B. Hospitality is also difficult because of individuals' attitudes.

    C. Hospitality is mistakenly regarded as lavish entertainent whose expense is traded off in the hope of gaining something.

IV. Christian hospitality is:

    A. Loving and serving the guest as Jesus loves and serves the host.

    B. Putting your resources at the disposal of others.

    C. A normal way of life.

    D. A way to welcome Jesus.

    E. Making your home a welcoming environment.

V. Hospitality can be learned.

    A. You can overcome obstacles based on pride and inadequacy.

        1. You have something to offer: Jesus' love and yours.

        2. Overcome protective attachment to your possessions.

        3. Use the time you have.

        4. Practice loving conversation.

    B. Observe and talk with those who are good hosts.

    C. Make a specific plan for hospitality in your household.

Discussion Starters

1. How have other people showed hospitality to you? What makes you feel comfortable in others' homes?

2. How have you experienced Jesus in receiving guests?

3. What practical things could you do to grow in hospitality?

4. How can we as a group extend hospitality to those who come to us as strangers?

"Homework"

1. Romans 12:1-18—Read the passage prayerfully. Meditate on v. 13. What implications does it have for you?
2. I Peter 4:7-11—Read the passage prayerfully. What gifts of yours can be put at the service of others (v. 10): material gifts, gifts of time, the gifts of listening, encouraging, exhorting . . .? Ask God to give you the gift of hospitality.
3. Where have you felt at home? What did your host do to make you comfortable?
4. Reflect on your experiences as host. What difficulties have you encountered? How have you been blessed in receiving guests? What has worked?
5. With your spouse or roommate(s), make a list of people to invite over for a meal or visit or overnight: relatives, Christian friends, pastor, associates from work or other organizations, neighbors. Think especially of people whose company may not be sought by others. Where is the Lord leading you to share him with others by opening up your home to them? Set up at least one occasion to receive one or more guests. If the time you try doesn't work, persist until you find one that does.
6. Matthew 9:35-10:20, 40-42—Read the passage prayerfully. How does it speak to you about being a visitor in others' homes? How can you be a better guest in others' homes? Make a list of people the Lord wants you to visit. Set up a time to visit at least one person.
7. Remember how you felt the first time you attended your church or prayer group. Did others make you welcome? What are you doing to welcome newcomers?

Servants of One Another
or
Business As Usual?

Talk Outline

Objective

To encourage the group to apply what they have learned in the course to their own situation.

Teacher Outline

I. Service is important in any Christian group.
    A. It carries out the gospel mandate.
    B. It frees others to do their job.
    C. It prevents spiritual stagnation.
    D. It binds believers together.
II. What kinds of service should you be doing?
    A. Individually
        1. Home and family.
        2. Work.
        3. Church or Christian organization.
        4. Other organizations.

    B. Corporately
       1. Serving the church or Christian organization.
       2. Reaching out to others.
          a. Sharing the gospel
          b. Serving the poor in corporal works of mercy.

III. Your Christian group needs to be organized for loving service.

    A. Pray together, expecting God's grace in your service.
    B. Designate leaders.
    C. Value every job and gift, not just the most visible ones.
    D. Specify jobs and expectations clearly.
    E. Talk together about difficulties you experience in serving.

IV. Cultivate the attitude of servants.

    A. Toward your work:
       1. Be eager to serve in any way.
       2. Commit yourself to do your job faithfully the best you can.
       3. Recognize that your service has spiritual value.
       4. Depend on the Spirit, not just your natural abilities.
    B. Toward others:
       1. Value each member of Christ's body.
       2. Commend and encourage others in their work.
       3. Refuse to argue, compete or criticize.
       4. Support the leader(s) by creative obedience.
       5. Treasure and seek unity.

Discussion Starters

1. How have you grown as a servant during this course? Where do you want to grow more?
2. What difficulties have you experienced in trying to serve?
3. How can we work together better?
4. Where do we go from here? Where does our parish/prayer group need service? How can we organize ourselves to meet that need?
5. Who outside of our group needs our service?
6. Do we want to meet again? When and why?

"Homework"

1. How have you grown as a servant through this course? What difficulties have you experienced and overcome? How have you experienced the Lord's presence giving you insight and wisdom, repentance and strength, love and support? Write a brief testimony of your experience in Servant School.
2. Read Acts 2:42-47, II Corinthians 8:1-5. How did those in the early church serve one another?
3. What concrete steps is the Lord calling you to take individually and corporately to continue growing in service love?